Half an Inch from the Edge

Half an Inch from the Edge

Teacher Education, Teaching, and Student Learning for Social Transformation

Noah Borrero, Patrick Roz Camangian,
Rick Ayers, Sharim Hannegan-Martinez,
and Esther Flores

ROWMAN & LITTLEFIELD
Lanham • Boulder • New York • London

Published by Rowman & Littlefield
An imprint of The Rowman & Littlefield Publishing Group, Inc.
4501 Forbes Boulevard, Suite 200, Lanham, Maryland 20706
https://rowman.com

6 Tinworth Street, London SE11 5AL, United Kingdom

Copyright © 2020 by Noah Borrero, Patrick Roz Camangian, Rick Ayers, Sharim Hannegan-Martinez, and Esther Flores

All rights reserved. No part of this book may be reproduced in any form or by any electronic or mechanical means, including information storage and retrieval systems, without written permission from the publisher, except by a reviewer who may quote passages in a review.

British Library Cataloguing in Publication Information Available

Library of Congress Cataloging-in-Publication Data

Library of Congress Control Number: 2019949257
ISBN 978-1-4758-3252-5 (cloth)
ISBN 978-1-4758-3255-6 (pbk.)
ISBN 978-1-4758-3262-4 (Electronic)

This book is dedicated to the UESJ Family. Thank you for being a part of this journey. We also want to send deep gratitude to all who contributed directly to this project: Abby Taheri-Woodworth, Bill Ayers, Bruna Lee, Carol Umanzor, Farima Pour-Khorshid, Gary Lew, and Vanessa Hernández.

Contents

Foreword		ix
Preface		xiii
Introduction: Socially Transformative Teaching: Disrupting White Supremacy		xvii
1	Notes to Mr. G: Making an Entirely New Story	1
2	Reflections on Mr. G: Humanizing Connections through Relevant Data	19
3	Autoethnographies with Esther: Building Community and Self-Discipline	27
4	Reflections on Esther: Assessment—Authentic versus Repressive	43
5	Reading the World and the Word with Sharim and Cam: The Power of Performance Poetry	57
6	Reflections on Sharim and Cam: Youth Voice, Student Literacies	67
7	Routines for Liberation with Ms. A: Classroom Community in Third Grade	73
8	Reflections on Ms. A: Revisiting the Purpose of Schooling	83
9	Socially Transformative Pedagogy and the Tasks for Urban Teachers	91
References		101
About the Authors		105

Foreword

Labels like "social justice" and "equity" have spread like wildfire across teacher education programs throughout the nation. While many programs pride themselves for utilizing these terms in their mission and vision statements, the ways in which they translate into practice continue to fail future educators and their students alike. Growing up as a student of color, I was often deeply frustrated by these disconnects within my K–12 schooling, as well as in my undergraduate and graduate level education programs. After teaching for over a decade within the same school district that I was a student in, as well as organizing within collectives such as the Teachers 4 Social Justice, the People's Education Movement, and the Education for Liberation Network, I learned valuable lessons about how schooling, spanning all levels of eduction, is disconnected to the humanity of people navigating school spaces. In my experiences as a professor within teacher education programs in California and in Nicaragua, I've had to grapple with the complexities of learning about social justice issues versus trying to teach for social justice. There are important and challenging questions that we must continue to ask ourselves as we work in solidarity with the next generation of social justice educators and this book allows readers to struggle with what it means to be teaching *half an inch from the edge.*

What does social justice look like in the everyday interactions, practices, policies, curriculum, relationships, and dynamics of teacher education programs and K–12 schools? Along these lines, whose voices are centered and which ones get marginalized in regard to programmatic issues? Who takes up more space in class discussions and who is silenced? How do teacher educators relate to student teachers' experiences within the field? And how do student teachers relate to K–12 students' experiences in schools? Which theories get prioritized and scaffolded for practice? What does critical literacy, racial literacy, and socioemotional literacy look like among teacher educators and among cooperating teachers with whom student teachers are paired with? And, are these various forms and levels of literacy that education stakeholders hold aligned with the integrity of the social justice mission(s) that the program purports to center? What does equity look like in terms of access to and distribution of support and resources? Issues like these are often the elephants in the room that critical educators question, see, and feel, but that regularly get swept under the guise of social justice slogans and rhetoric.

As a former adjunct instructor and current first-year tenure track professor within the urban education and social justice (UESJ) program, I can speak to the intentionality that I've witnessed and experienced firsthand throughout my years of service at the University of San Francisco. UESJ, from my vantage point, has been unapologetic in its commitment to not only recruit and accept students from historically marginalized backgrounds, but to do the same in the ways they recruit and support adjuncts and faculty of color. With this kind of commitment comes great responsibility and sacrifice that mainstream teacher preparation programs tend to overlook. While the efforts of UESJ to support students committed to social justice has not been perfect, what I appreciate most is the program leaders' relentless commitment to learn from mistakes and to continue to build and grow from these important lessons. I cannot stress how important it is for teacher educators to model humility especially in the messiness of this work, to show students just how imperfect we are, especially when we are trying to practice "what we preach." There is so much value in understanding our "unfinishedness" and our collective ongoing need to heal from what bell hooks names as our "imperialist, capitalist, white supremacist patriarchy," which impacts us all, regardless of how critically conscious we believe ourselves to be. This level of commitment was birthed through many failed attempts to enact social justice pedagogy in teacher education. Rather than covering up these failed attempts, both UESJ students and professors have courageously centered the elephants in the room because of our collective love for justice and commitment to education for liberation. Most times centering the elephants in the room results in uncomfortable, emotional, and transformative moments for both student teachers and their teacher educators alike. It was and still is through these kinds of moments that we shift and contribute to an ever-evolving vision and movement for justice.

The amazing teacher and teacher educator voices featured in this book help readers to demystify what teaching for social justice looks and feels like, across various contexts. Reading each chapter offers us a window to see the challenges and beauty of attempting to bridge theory to practice. The reality is that we cannot afford to romanticize or sanitize teaching for social justice in the dangerous times that we are still navigating since colonization. It is our duty to push back, to reimagine, and to reclaim education with and for our communities. The political and moral clarity that is needed in the field of education can only be as strong as the hearts that are committed to humility, justice, and vulnerability, which are all necessary to sharpen analyses and our practices. I have so much respect and deep gratitude for educators that are committed to living justice out loud, like the contributors of this book in their respective chapters, which is always inspiring and activating. Our justice work does not start and end in the classroom because we are activists and organizers inside *and* outside of schools.

Dr. Farima Pour-Khorshid
University of San Francisco

Preface

We are teachers. As a group, we've taught in K–12 public school classrooms for over thirty years. We care deeply about our educational system, our teacher colleagues, and especially the young people in our schools. Recognizing the important work of teaching, we have to look squarely at an education system that was set up to reproduce hierarchies, that has continued white supremacy and patriarchy under the guise of meritocracy.

And while we are deeply troubled by the current political leadership in our country and its consistent and sustained attack on public education, we recognize that schools are one of the main sites of contention in our society, one of the places where we fight over and work out what kind of world we want to live in. Because we work closely with teachers and young people, we remain hopeful that US public schools can be robust sites for imagining and constructing a future that works, places that recognize the humanity and worth of each person and community.

Additionally, we are all teacher educators. We are privileged to work alongside new colleagues as they enter the profession, and we're energized and enlightened every day by the passion, creativity, and commitment they bring to the field and into the classroom. Too much is written about education from the outside, from the lofty and remote perch of the academy, the think tank, or the foundation. In this book, we showcase the ingenuity of new teachers, their actual practice of inventing, improvising, and working out socially transformative education.

Along with these profiles, we reflect a critical analysis of our current public education system. In this portrayal resides a deep and powerful tension—K–12 classrooms are sites of great possibility and tremendous oppression. While our system may work for some, it historically and continuously silences and derails others. This tension lies at the heart of teaching—particularly for new teachers of color working in historically targeted communities where the forces of structural inequity can be overwhelming. We present classroom-based examples from four new teachers to show that meaningful, culturally relevant and sustaining teaching is present—and thriving—in K–12 classrooms despite the pressures working against it. We build upon the concept of cultural relevance in an attempt to show that socially transformative pedagogy—teaching that centers the lived experiences of youth to provide opportunities to make positive change in their own communities—is a process that involves struggle, humility, and a deep sense of caring for young people.

The case studies that are at the core of this book are not lifted up as exemplars of perfect classrooms or flawless curricular interventions. They are varied, personal, and remarkable portraits of the messiness that critical, asset-based teaching entails. And, as important, they represent the deeply self-reflective work of four new teachers who refuse to buy into an educational narrative and current in this country that prioritizes testing over learning. These portraits remind us that there is no formula for "best practices," no going to scale, no mandates from above that make for good teaching. Instead, it is the critical consciousness and deep commitment of these teachers, and others who work from the ground up, that allows them to invent and sustain their everyday successes.

The pedagogical and political stance that these teachers take is embodied in their classroom teaching, and it is what gives us hope for and pride in the work we do as teachers and teacher educators. Each of these four new teachers—Mr. G., Esther, Sharim, and Abby Taheri-Woodworth—are graduates of the urban education and social justice (UESJ) program at the University of San Francisco (USF)—a two-year combined masters/credential program in California. UESJ is a cohort stream within the university teacher education department, one dedicated to recruiting and sustaining critical teachers of color as well as training white teachers to act in solidarity (not "service") as engaged allies.

The UESJ project itself has been a living thing, learning and growing and figuring out how to take next steps. Developing out of the Center for Teaching Excellence and Social Justice founded at USF by Herb Kohl, UESJ has focused on recruiting organizers and community-based activists into the profession. Many of our teachers have themselves struggled in school; some have received low grades; others have been suspended or expelled. Part of their drive to teach has been powered by those defeats: I'll go back on a mission of reparation. I'll go back and become the teacher I wish I'd had in my youth.

In the process of their teacher preparation, everyone in UESJ planted a seed for their pedagogy through a classroom-based action research project and thesis during their time in the program. In this book, we explore this journey of young educators as they extend the possibilities for socially transformative pedagogy through this type of learning as teacher-scholars.

We don't present UESJ as a panacea for teacher education. We know that there is no such thing. Teaching is a lifelong endeavor and there is no preparation better than spending time in classrooms with youth. But as we reflect on the first ten years of UESJ—envisioning, developing, implementing, and refining a new program—we believe we are learning important lessons that must be shared. Just like the teachers' projects in the case studies of this book, the program itself is a work in progress. It's a struggle—rife with failure and second attempts. And, like the classroom-based research projects themselves, UESJ marks a starting point—a beginning of reflection, dialogue, and teaching in the journey toward social transformation.

Introduction

*Socially Transformative Teaching:
Disrupting White Supremacy*

Teachers and activists doing powerful work in classrooms today are challenging the racist deficit narrative that blames youth for their marginalization in schools. Let us not accept that "educated" is a one-dimensional attainment. It is crucial to reframe the problem, asking "education for whom? education for what?" Students in historically dispossessed, underresourced, overexploited, and underserved communities do not simply need to get initiated into white-centered epistemologies, into middle class discourse, or into the current demands of corporations.

Instead, students must be given the freedom and creativity to imagine the kind of world their communities need and the steps necessary to build those communities. This is education for liberation, by which we mean developing the skills and experiences to transform one's social circumstances. Socially transformative pedagogy is the educational project that youth need today.

This book provides four case studies of early career teachers by exploring their teacher action research projects and their subsequent classroom lives. These cases suggest a reframing of the current narrative on K–12 public education to focus more purposefully on the reality that is the opportunity gap prevalent in urban schools. Instead of highlighting what students of color lack (e.g., compliant behavior and dominant vernacular English), the focus must be on the ways that urban youth have had disproportionately less access to an equitable education and how to make such an education possible.

Furthermore, the case studies illustrate teachers' self-reflective journeys towards socially transformative pedagogies and highlight important teacher training constructs of the urban education and social justice (UESJ) program at the University of San Francisco.

As it stands, students of color in urban schools overwhelmingly experience irrelevant curriculum and poorly trained, impersonal teachers. These learning conditions are major contributors to the sense of academic marginalization and social alienation that ultimately results in the high disappearance rates—commonly referred to as dropout rates—of students of color from school.

LEARNING FROM STUDENTS

Prospective teachers in the University of San Francisco's (USF) program in UESJ masters and teaching credential are encouraged to think about the ways that schools and teaching must fundamentally change before issues like the disappearance rate of students of color from schools can be addressed. Alumna Charley Brooks explained during her first semester in the two-year program: "I don't think I understood the root causes of the problem . . . Viewing the achievement gap as a gap is continuing to think about our students as inept, or dysfunctional, or having a deficit; rather than seeing it as a systemic issue."

Similarly, Brooks' cohort-mate, Irene Rohrs, echoed that "the reason there's a gap has a lot to do with the way people look at urban students. . . . They genuinely think that they're not doing well in school because they're not trying hard enough. But [in this program] we're learning how to really see the bigger picture."

While we have sought to teach our diverse cohorts of early-career, critical teachers, we find that they have taught us so much more as they have gone out to schools and critically applied what it means to engage in social justice teaching. They have practiced first-hand implementing socially transformative pedagogy in their classrooms.

In these pages, we examine the actual practice of teaching by focusing on the day-to-day classrooms where our teachers are making a difference, by framing the big picture issues and challenges in schools today. Prior to beginning their careers in urban schools, new teachers often fall short of understanding the degree to which youth of color in urban communities are underserved. It is not until new teachers are faced with the challenges of dealing with conflicts in the classroom without the proper training that they begin to truly understand systemic disparities.

Rather than focus exclusively on instructional methods, the UESJ program attempts to prepare teachers to be much more responsive to the needs of urban students. For example, students develop collaborative, community-based action research projects through which they apply critical educational theory within the realities of urban schools and communities. These research projects will be the focus of the case studies in this book.

Students in the UESJ program learn a new and more democratic principle of accountability: an accountability to the communities they serve. They learn a new and more effective metaphor for teaching—not of the missionary bestowing gifts but of an organizer working alongside students and communities for justice.

Teacher candidates in the UESJ program also confront the culturally biased perspective that views the realities and struggles of urban youth as apart from, if not irrelevant to, a rigorous academic program. Accordingly, UESJ candidates work to create curricula that reflect the ways urban youth experience the harsh conditions of their everyday lives. Doing so requires teachers to not see their sole presence in urban schools itself as transformative.

The UESJ program begins with the work of identifying and recruiting preservice teachers from communities that are similar to the ones they seek to serve. Candidates then engage in a critical level of self-analysis and self-reflection in order to develop as organizer-teachers. The value of this practice is named by Rohrs who said, "teachers come into urban schools thinking it's charity work, but then there's people here who come into it knowing it's a way of life. Not just a career, but a life choice . . . Having people from the communities we end up going back to teach . . . just makes it less academic and more, just, real life."

Indeed, alumna Kristia Castrillo added, "Studying with other people who come from, and work in similar communities that I do, allows me to see that the problems are really similar in a lot of communities of color, but that there are also different ways we can address the needs of our youth." The purposeful recruitment and enrollment of culturally diverse candidates leads to more honest, authentic conversations dealing with issues of social justice and injustice.

These conversations require humility, deep listening, and respect; they serve a useful function in creating a collective identity among candidates in the cohort. Alumnus Richard Bennett reflected on the importance of collective identity when saying, "Looking back [on the program], there's a strong sense of community, and people who share a common belief in the brilliance of every child in our communities." In developing this identity and purpose together, these early career teachers learn ways to counter the deficit perspective that pushes so many students out of our schools. They begin to see their own teaching as a way to change the system.

Introduction

URBAN SCHOOLS AND THE MYTH OF ACHIEVEMENT

Culturally relevant teaching is important in all schooling contexts—urban, rural, and suburban. All students deserve great teachers and access to quality educational opportunities that foster their lived experiences. The focus of this book is socially transformative pedagogy in urban classrooms and the need to address the structural inequities and deficit labels that plague students and teachers in urban schools.

This book explores what the word "urban" has come to denote in public education, and the fact that descriptors like "diverse" and "minority" are statistically inaccurate in many urban districts. This analysis highlights the importance of socially transformative pedagogy in urban schools because of the growing cultural divide between teachers and students and the need for teachers to study, acknowledge, and harness the cultural assets that students bring with them to school.

For example, contemporary learning theories show that students are continually learning within and across different cultural contexts, yet teachers too often separate classroom learning from learning that is happening in students' homes or among peers. For urban students, the navigation of multiple—and often competing—cultural contexts needs to be utilized as a cultural asset that connects to classroom learning. This connection is at the heart of socially transformative pedagogy.

When thinking about urban schools, Jay MacLeod's (1987) *Ain't No Makin' It* provides a basic understanding of educational inequity and equity in the American educational system. This undergraduate thesis—turned into a book—replicated a study by Catholic priest and social scientist Paul Willis (1977) in *Learning to Labour*, which explained how school disruption by working class youth was an affirmative stance of resistance, expressing community agency against an institution that was not in their interest.

In his study, MacLeod added the variable of race in an urban US city to understand the relationship between achievement, social class, and education. And here again, resistance was found to be an affirmative decision rather than an inborn failure. Both of their studies had similar archetypes: MacLeod's "Hallway Hangers" were similarly disengaged with school as Willis's "Lads" because they saw school as subtractive to their identities, while MacLeod's "Brothers" and Willis's "Ear'oles" were engaged with school and saw it as their ticket out of poverty.

MacLeod and Willis initially found that the Hallway Hangers and Lads had a nihilistic view of life, focused on themselves, and were absorbed in what they were going through in their personal lives. These were the reasons that they were failing in schools. Conversely, MacLeod and Willis found the Brothers and Ear'oles were compliant, followed orders, followed instructions, did their homework on time, paid attention in class, and so forth. Those were the reasons they were more successful.

Both researchers concluded that the Hallway Hangers and Lads had an oppositional identity toward schooling, which was tied to what we might think of today as a culture of poverty: it was a way of living that supposedly contributed to the reasons people were poor. This oppositional identity and cultural poverty essentially led to a social reproduction of poverty in their lives, their families' lives, and in their community.

What Paul Willis did not ask, but MacLeod did is this: If you actually do better in school, does that in fact translate into economic opportunity? MacLeod decided to revisit the site and subjects of his study eight years later and found, essentially, that the Hallway Hangers were right—that even if one complied and was academically engaged, doing so did not guarantee an economic shift in a person's quality of life.

Compliance did not necessarily mean that students navigating their way out of poverty would have the same opportunity as wealthier students who get the same grades and go to the same universities, for example. A lot of MacLeod's Brothers who complied in high school went to universities and experienced culture shock and other incongruences with university life. They were pushed out, sent back to the communities they came from, and took jobs in local industries. The Hallway Hangers, who took similar jobs two or three years prior to the Brothers, were now their bosses.

From this perspective, MacLeod's study provided empirical data that meritocracy was a myth. In so doing, it disrupted achievement ideologies that one earns success through hard work, grit, and education because it illustrated that even when poor kids worked the system, there was no guarantee of upward mobility. These ideologies—compounded by the deficit perspectives that blame urban youth for their lack of achievement—continue to reproduce an educational system that is structurally inequitable.

MacLeod's research demonstrates that schools are selling a pipe dream, and only a few who buy the tickets will actually get into the show. His research suggests that conforming to schooling is no guarantee for upward mobility. The implications of MacLeod's findings are important to remember when educators are faced with meritocratic narratives and achievement ideologies used to place accountability for economic well-being and blame for a lack of upward mobility primarily on those who are underserved by social systems that are unequal by design. Instead, MacLeod's study gives credence to understanding that poverty in most ways is systemic.

However, much of the dominating mainstream discourse places the blame for poverty on those who experience its harsh realities—especially urban youth and their families. There are numerous examples of the varied and compounding aspects of the discourse of deficit and the "culture of poverty."

For example, one of the leading consultants for schools educating students of color is Ruby Payne (2005, 2001), whose *A Framework for Understanding Poverty* and *Bridges Out of Poverty* are used by districts across the country to support teachers in understanding their students. Payne argues that the problem with poor kids, which explains their inability to do well in school among other things, is that they cannot delay gratification. They have a present-time orientation and they do not have a good enough future orientation.

Payne centers the problem on a supposed culture and values for poor students—especially students of color. They devalue education and learning and have a high tolerance for antisocial behavior. Her perspective, which aligns comfortably with the world view of the oppressor, suggests that there is a pathology of poverty, that the "other" needs to be fixed.

American comedian and cultural icon Bill Cosby, before he was brought down by the exposure of his own horrible sexual assaults, provides another example of the insidious discourse surrounding poverty. Cosby delivered the infamous Pound Cake speech at a NAACP commemoration for the fiftieth anniversary of the *Brown versus the Board of Education* Supreme Court decision, where he started talking about the problem with black children by saying,

> They're standing on the corner and they can't speak English. I can't even talk the way these people talk: Why you ain't,' Where you is' . . . And I blamed the kid until I heard the mother talk. And then I heard the father talk . . . Everybody knows it's important to speak English except these knuckleheads . . . With names like Shaniqua, Taliqua and Mohammed and all of that crap, and all of them are in jail. Brown versus the Board of Education is no longer the white person's problem. (2004)

Upon criticism of his comments a few days later, he further remarked, "They think they're hip . . . They can't read; they can't write. They're laughing and giggling, and they're going nowhere."

Finally, President Donald Trump's Housing and Urban Development Secretary Ben Carson reinforced that narrative, suggesting that "poverty to a large extent is also a state of mind." The point here being that the fault is in the oppressed, not in the structures that hold them down.

These are just a few examples of the hatred and othering of dispossessed and marginalized communities in our country. Each of these dominant perspectives start off by framing problems with poor children, people, and communities rather than identifying the root causes for the challenges that poor children face. These deficit-oriented narratives focus on what these targeted youth supposedly cannot do, instead of looking to solutions.

These narratives are also deficit-oriented because they blame poor and oppressed people for the oppression that they experience without acknowledging that their lived experiences are shaped by the material conditions in their lives. At the root of these perspectives—and something often unnamed—is a deep disdain for dispossessed, overexploited, and underserved communities. And this disdain is continually reinforced and deepened by those in positions of power.

BARRIERS CREATED BY WHITE PRIVILEGE IN EDUCATION

The culture of power in schools is firmly rooted in white, Eurocentric norms. And these norms impact all aspects of student learning—from the curriculum they are taught, to the proficiency levels they are supposed to strive towards, to the teachers in front of them. For example, according to the National Center for Educational Statistics (2018), 84 percent of the public teaching force is white—and the vast majority of them are middle class.

Hyland's (2000) research found that most teachers, regardless of race, described themselves as effective teachers of predominantly low-income and working class students of color. In a study of 222 teachers in a highly rated, Midwestern school district, Kailin (1999) found that most white teachers, amidst slogans of "excellence," "tolerance," and "success for all," (p. 747) blamed the causes and perpetuation of racism on blacks, despite remaining silent and not challenging racist behavior they witnessed from white colleagues.

For Wilson (1970), this rhetorical practice "protects the professional educator's self-esteem at the expense of the children; protects the educator's status at the expense of the community's interests . . . protects the middle class from competition with those who they feel aren't ready . . ." (p. 307). According to Feagin and Vera (1995), these are "socially organized set[s] of attitudes, ideas, and practices that deny African Americans and other People of color the dignity, opportunities, freedoms, and rewards that this nation offers white Americans" (p. 7).

These practices result in experienced racism from teachers like these in schools throughout the country, serving to keep white teachers in positions of power and students of color in positions of powerlessness. This further reinforces the disdain for the oppressed by oppressor and alienation from school that students (and teachers) of color experience.

McIntosh (1988) refers to this phenomenon as a matter of *white privilege*, "an invisible package of unearned assets that [whites] can count on cashing in each day, but about which [they are] 'meant' to remain oblivious" (p. 61). Her confessional account of her white privilege in racially stratified America serves as a model process for white teachers to overcome any white guilt that may disrupt their process to humbly recognize ways they overlook the struggles of students of color. Once white teachers admit to their privilege in a racially stratified society, they become open to the possibility of engaging in antiracist, cross-racial solidarity.

According to Leonardo (2004), however, "White guilt blocks [this] critical reflection because Whites end up feeling individually blameworthy for racism. In fact, they become overly concerned with whether or not they 'look racist' and forsake the more central project of understanding the contours of structural racism" (p. 140). If they are not owning up to these tensions, white teachers are less prepared to utilize teaching practices that join them with their students against racial injustice.

When they fail to understand the sociopolitical context of urban education, white teachers continue to perpetuate a deficit-based approach to teaching that harms urban youth of color by failing to recognize the cultural strengths that students have and bring to school every day.

Increasing the teacher of color workforce, moreover, does not guarantee that student achievement will increase for non-white urban youth. Despite a bulk of studies centered on white teachers' racial attitudes in urban communities of color, many teachers of color also subscribe to notions of white supremacy in schools when they view their students through a deficit thinking model that "contends that minority cultural values, as transmitted through the family, are dysfunctional, and therefore cause low educational and occupational attainment" (Solórzano & Yosso, 2001, p. 6).

While there is a lack of empirical research investigating the negative impact of white supremacy by teachers of color on students of color, classic antiracist educational theories by Freire (1970) and Woodson (1933) are applicable here. Identifying with the humanity of their oppressors, Freire argued that the oppressed (teachers) "internalized the image of the oppressor and adopted his guidelines" (p. 31). According to Woodson, "Negroes . . . [who] serve their race as teachers . . . are powerless . . . miseducated [and of] no service to themselves" (pp. 22–23).

Capitulation of teachers of color into a racist paradigm makes them no longer servants to their communities; instead, teaching with internalized racial self-hatred positions them as servants of a social system that is at odds with the racial uplift for people of color. And it is this cycle, too, that contributes to the narrative of a culture of poverty in our educational system.

As echoed in the statements from new teachers at the start of this introduction, teachers often enter the profession with the best of intentions to support urban youth, yet they have limited opportunities to develop a critical social analysis of the factors impacting urban communities and schools.

Violence and consumption are not inherent to communities of color. Instead, these coping mechanisms are responses to the history of systemic harm that has been imposed on these communities and internalized as appropriate responses to their social conditions given the limited options open to them.

Women also continue to struggle against the tumultuous evolution of urban misogyny and rape culture—which are systemic and endemic of the "nation's political system" of "imperialist white-supremacist capitalist patriarchy" (hooks, 2010, p. 2). Youth of color are being systematically targeted for their purchasing power by commercial media while schools are slow to adopt critical media literacy teaching practices that pay closer attention to developing consciousness to prepare students of color to deal with highly materialistic media narratives on their own. In spite of all of the ways that youth of color are targeted and violated, by and large teachers do not understand the realities of their students' lives.

LOOKING FORWARD

Highlighting the challenges outlined in this introduction is crucial to better understanding how UESJ sees the role of teachers and teacher educators committed to urban schools. These challenges not only showcase the contextual forces pushing against the country's public schools, but they also help name the historical and structural failures of a larger society. The chapters to come will also adopt this systemic approach in their exploration of urban public schools. The work with teachers who strive to understand these larger structural forces and combat them through their pedagogy provides critical hope that this country's urban public schools can be sites of transformation. This process of continual learning is at the heart of socially transformative pedagogy that UESJ seeks to employ and develop alongside new teachers.

KEY IDEAS IN THIS CHAPTER

- This book focuses on urban schools and the need to shift the discourse from what urban students and students of color lack to what assets and unique experiences they bring to the classroom.
- In order to enact a socially transformative pedagogy in their classrooms, teachers must first and foremost understand the historical and systemic inequities that have plagued students in urban communities.
- Seeing urban schools as places of transformation and resistance is at the core of socially transformative pedagogy.

Chapter One

Notes to Mr. G

Making an Entirely New Story

The notes in the journal are carefully shaped, in fifth grade scrawl: "When I grow up, I want to be a gamer. To be a Minecraft gamer to be exact. I want to be a Minecraft gamer because I have experience in Pocket Edition. My brother has Minecraft on his phone. I built a huge house." On the next page is a full-page drawing of a superhero-like cartoon character she created named "Budder"; a block-shaped hero wearing sunglasses, equipped with a sword made from butter.

Next is a note back from the teacher. No correction of grammar or punctuation. No praise or criticism; just this:

> Budder? So this is a character made of butter? And he throws bricks of butter at people and has a buttery sword?! That buttery sword would be so cool to have! Imagine slicing bread with it! You would already be buttering it while you slice it! I would want a character like that. Oh! And he can have like a flame sword too! One to toast the bread and one to butter it! Great Idea Kaitlyn!

How does this light-hearted exchange and others contribute to a project of radical, socially transformative teaching? This freeform literacy practice brought a classroom to life in the case study of "Notes to Mr. G."

MR. G'S TEACHING CONTEXT

Mr. G is a fifth grade teacher at a public school in the Chinatown neighborhood of San Francisco. He is Chinese American, born and raised in San

Francisco, and views his work as a new teacher as a way to be a part of and give back to his community. Prior to starting his career as a teacher, he worked for three years in the restaurant business. He credits this time, working in the real world, dedication, and customer service as vital in the formation of his desires to become a teacher and the vision of the teacher he wants to become: involved with the community and working with kids.

In his own words, Mr. G reflected on the ways in which his work in the restaurant industry impacts his vision of teaching:

> With first-hand experience in seeing how attention to detail and being able to meet the needs of each customer are key ingredients to success in the food service industry, I have tried to apply those same concepts within the classroom setting.
>
> Attention to detail in the food industry can be broken down into three key aspects: consistency, flavor, and presentation. In terms of school, these three aspects greatly influence how your students view you. As a teacher, are you a positive role model that your students can look up to? Can they rely on you when they truly need you? Consistency as a teacher is determined by how you choose to characterize yourself.
>
> In terms of flavor, what sets you apart as a teacher? What sorts of unique perspectives and experiences can you provide to your students to have them see the world in a different light? In the restaurant industry, the uniqueness of flavor and its authenticity are what sets apart a decent establishment from a great one.
>
> As for presentation, what can we do as teachers to pique our students' interests? Are the lessons we design for them engaging? Do they cater to their senses of smell, touch, taste, hearing, and sight? Is what they learn in the classroom something that can spark their imaginations?
>
> But on top of all this, one thing to keep in mind is if what we are teaching to our students is palatable? Is what we are teaching to them relevant? Is it something they can comprehend and apply to their daily lives? As elaborate as we can design a lesson for them, is it also useful? Because, what good is a meal that looks, smells, and tastes wonderful, but doesn't fulfill the most basic of needs? Nourishment. As a person who has had experience in the kitchen, this is how the restaurant experience has influenced my positionality as an aspiring classroom teacher.

Mr. G wrote the passage above during his student teaching semester, and it reflects aspects of his personality and creativity as a teacher and the unique experiences and expectations of his growth as a teacher.

Mr. G utilizes his personality and creativity as assets in his pedagogy. For example, while his classroom is not a part of the bilingual program at the school, he uses his Cantonese to connect with students and families and to support monolingual teachers on site. Further, as one of only three male teachers on the faculty, he is the first male teacher that many of his students have had in their school careers to date. As a San Francisco native, he tries to bring a sense of pride and appreciation for the community that was a part of his K–12 experience.

Mr. G's school is one of the largest and oldest elementary schools in the city, with more than 600 students in grades K–5 and with a history going back some 150 years. Historically, this site was known as one of the only elementary schools that allowed Chinese Americans to attend, and it was a part of important legislative and political action striving for equitable access to education for students learning English. The site is located in the center of a bustling commercial area and the majority of students live in the surrounding community.

Mr. G's school currently serves a student population of whom 90 percent identify as Asian American (the vast majority of whom identify as Chinese American). Of this population, more than 90 percent qualify for free or reduced lunch and more than 70 percent are classified as English language learners. Mr. G's fifth grade class reflects these larger demographic descriptors and is one of two non–Cantonese-English bilingual fifth-grade classes.

MR. G'S PERSPECTIVES ON SOCIALLY TRANSFORMATIVE PEDAGOGY

Mr. G is a connector. He is interested in creating meaningful relationships and doing the work to build a sense of community. As an urban education and social justice (UESJ) student earning his teaching credential, this meant that Mr. G was eager to learn from and with his classmates, and he was often the one organizing social gatherings beyond the classroom context. He thrived on this sense of community and continually expressed his gratitude for being a part of a cohort of teachers who traveled through their graduate studies together. As a teacher, this meant that Mr. G was truly invested in building a sense of community in his classroom and developing a pedagogy centered on trust and respect.

Upon entering his graduate program, Mr. G was the first to admit that his background and foundations in educational theory, critical social analysis, and social justice pedagogy were limited. He attended local public schools, wanted to be a positive influence in the community, and was completely dedicated to teaching as his career. However, his attention to issues of race, class, gender, and heteronormativity within public education were just being developed. Mr. G's respect for and appreciation of colleagues with such perspectives were foundational in his learning. For example, he reflected on their influence on his overall approach to becoming a teacher: "One thing that I am sure of is that being a member of [this] cohort has had the greatest impact."

Central to Mr. G's learning and a major focus of his approach as a new teacher is based on attention to relationship-building. He wants to learn as much as possible about each of his students, and his primary job as a teacher is to connect the learning that he is doing to the content he is teaching. As a new teacher, Mr. G is quickly confronting the complexities involved in truly learning about students. He is balancing the district-reported test scores and reading levels of his students with his own interactions in the classroom.

He is learning that data he receives about students from the district do not even begin to tell a story about his learners. And he sees the impact that testing (and test scores) has on students and teachers' perspectives of them. He relates this view back to his own K–12 experiences, and how test scores and passing grades were valued over all else at school.

Mr. G often talks about the fact that his own schooling was not centered around relationships—he remembers a focus on good grades and compliant behavior. He also shares that this is what many of his current students express regarding the expectations their parents have of them.

The sense of pressure that accompanies such expectations is something that Mr. G discusses as a part of his schooling and a harsh reality for many of his students. He sees his work—especially as an elementary school teacher—to support students academically and socially by connecting to them, sharing from his own experiences, and working with them to move beyond a focus on grades and behavior—to share in a quest for lifelong learning. And as a part of this, he sees the need to move beyond the limits of tests and grades in assessing his students.

Foundational in this process is Mr. G's desire to authentically learn from, with, and about his students. He is interested in their lives and wants to create meaningful learning experiences for them in his classroom. To do so, he creates informal assessments that purposefully reach beyond tests and worksheets to expand notions of literacy. As will be seen in Mr. G's journaling project and in the accompanying analysis provided in chapter 2, cultivating culturally relevant data is a foundational aspect of socially transformative pedagogy.

JOURNALING IN MR. G'S CLASS

One aspect of Mr. G's teaching that showcases his relational approach to teaching and his attention to culturally relevant data collection is a yearlong interactive journaling project that he titles "Notes to Mr. G." Each student has a journal and the weekly prompts are designed for students to write freely on a given topic. Mr. G works to collect the journals biweekly to read students' responses and provide some writing of his own in response to their ideas.

The objectives of "Notes to Mr. G" center on relationship-building and student self-expression through writing. Mr. G strives to build relationships through these interactive journals by providing accessible and creative prompts for students and then sharing parts of his own life via his own writing in student journals. He views the journals and student writing as part of a way to learn about students, engage in written dialogue with them, and build a sense of classroom culture—a process that he develops alongside his students.

Just like the relationships they are building as student and teacher, the journal is an opportunity for students to share aspects of their lives (without worrying about being graded) and for Mr. G to offer ideas, reflections, and interests of his own through the prompts and his own writing back to students. Further, he uses the journals as a way to connect other classroom content with students' personal interests and experiences.

For young writers, "Notes to Mr. G" is an opportunity to write freely, creatively, and personally in a classroom context. While Mr. G does not formally grade students' entries or correct for grammar and spelling, for example, he is continually using them as opportunities to glimpse into students' interests and worldviews while also formatively assessing students' literacy skills.

KEY ASPECTS OF "NOTES TO MR. G"

Given the interactive nature of "Notes to Mr. G" and its focus on building relationships between the student and teacher, it is ideally a classroom project that begins early in the school year. Mr. G provides a spiral-bound notebook for each student and introduces "Notes to Mr. G" by utilizing class time for students to personally design their own journal cover. Students use markers and crayons along with magazines, scissors, and glue to cut out images and design a journal that they feel is their own.

As students design their journals and as a part of this introduction, Mr. G writes key elements of the project on the board: "This journal is yours to keep. You and I will be the only ones who write in this journal. Your writing in this journal will not be graded."

When students complete designing their journal covers, Mr. G provides an overview of "Notes to Mr. G" by referring to the three statements on the board. He begins by emphasizing that it is very important for him to get to know students—as writers, as readers, as thinkers, and as people. He talks about literacy—how people read the world—and how journaling is a way to reflect on experiences. He expresses wanting to learn about their interests, ideas, goals, and lives outside of the classroom. He also says that he wants students to learn about him and feel free to ask him questions about his life.

Mr. G explains that the goals of the journals are to practice writing and to learn about each other. He says that journals will be used weekly (mostly on Fridays) and are not meant to be a test, but rather a way of communicating with each other throughout the school year. Prompts will range from fun topics, to serious topics, to current events, to classroom- and school-based issues. The only rule is that students write during the time provided (or the time assigned for homework). There is no wrong answer as a long as there is a written response to the journal prompt.

Mr. G then discusses how he will collect journals on every second Friday, read them, and provide a written response to something he has read. He says that his goal in doing so is to develop a written conversation with each student through the journals. His responses are not meant to be answers or judgments, but rather as ways of talking to one another through the journals. Students can choose if they want to write more in response to his writing in their journals. He ends by asking students if there are any questions about "Notes to Mr. G."

He then writes the first journal prompt and gives students ten minutes to write freely during class time. This first prompt is one that all students can access and is open ended. Examples can range from "Describe how it feels to be a fifth grader. Why do you feel this way?" to "How do you describe yourself as a writer? Why? What are some examples of things you have written in the past?"

Following this first writing activity, Mr. G has a student collect the journals and put them in a designated place in the classroom—a place where all students can see them, use them during free time, and refer to them when needed. He explains that they will typically write "Notes to Mr. G" on Fridays, but there may be other opportunities to write. He says that students are free to take journals home if they would like to write more, but the journals need to be back in their special place on Fridays.

On the second Friday of the school year, Mr. G takes the journals home with him, reads selected student writing, and provides a comment or question for each student to consider when journals are returned the following week. Like the types of feedback suggested by Nancy Atwell (1987), these comments and questions are not evaluative, but rather are intended to share something that Mr. G knows his students don't know about him. These can range from expressing his fears about his own writing, to memories he has from fifth grade, to a question directly related to what a student has written. Ideally, each comment provides opportunity for students to reply in writing if they so desire.

Mr. G is constantly using the journals as a form of data collection. While students are writing in class, he is moving around the room and connecting with individual students to learn about their writing skills—what helps them get started, their penmanship, how much they write in a given amount of time, and so forth. Further, as he is reading their journals, he is learning about their use of language, their mechanics, and the depth of their thinking about different topics. Most importantly, he is learning about students—their hobbies, interests, critical thinking, senses of humor, fears, anxieties, passions, and ways of reading their own worlds as fifth graders. And to push his engagement with students and what he is learning about them, he responds—in writing—about the things he finds intriguing and impressionable.

Journal prompts range from open-ended reflective writing (e.g., "What changes do you notice in your local community?"), to writing about current events (e.g., "What do you think about President Trump's plan to build a wall at the US—Mexico border? Why?"), to fun ideas that might come up in class (e.g., "If we were to have a class pet, what should it be and why?"), to issues that are impacting students at school (e.g., the entire fifth grade had recess taken away due to bullying on the yard; he asked students to write an action plan about how bullying should be addressed at school). As the school year progresses, prompts also connect directly to classroom content and to the development of students' critical thinking. He continually assesses students' engagement in different curricular units and uses his comments and questions to urge students to think about how they can apply their learning in their lives outside of the classroom.

At the end of each term, Mr. G uses the journals as a tool for students to reflect on their writing and thinking throughout the time period, and he uses his final journal collection as a time to reflect on their growth as writers and thinkers. The culminating assignment asks students to look back through their writing over the course of the school year to think about some of the things they have learned about themselves, Mr. G, and being a fifth grader.

MR. G'S ACTION RESEARCH

Given Mr. G's experiences as a student in local public schools and his focus on building relationships through culturally relevant data, he developed "Notes to Mr. G" as a classroom intervention to address the research question, "How can interactive journaling impact student-teacher connections?" As an action researcher, this question came from his experiences as a student in which all classroom writing was seen as evaluative and part of a larger, monolithic focus on grades, achievement, and academic success—none of which seemed to involve or include his interests, creativity, or life outside of school.

Mr. G's burgeoning experiences with his own fifth graders (and many of their parents) reinforced this distancing of self or identity from school learning for students and the need for teachers to make classroom learning more real and more relevant. From this perspective, he framed his action research by stating this:

> The problem that needs to be addressed within our schools is the disconnect in communication that exists between students and teachers. Kincheloe (2008) gives an example where "a district supervisor who writes a curriculum in social studies, for example, that demands the simple transference of a body of established facts about the great men and great events of American history is also teaching a political lesson that upholds the status quo"; but in doing so leaves "no room for students or teachers in such a curriculum to explore alternate sources, to compare diverse historical interpretations, to do research for their own and produce knowledge that may conflict with prevailing interpretations" (p. 9).

In thinking of "Notes to Mr. G" as a way to begin to address this disconnect in communication, Mr. G utilized theoretical frameworks that centered on student investment and authentic caring. He framed student investment as a contrast to student engagement by placing the onus on teachers and the need to invest in student success through the development of an approach to data collection that values students' diverse backgrounds and learning styles.

Mr. G framed authentic caring as the work of teachers to not only care about students' academic learning in various content areas, but to learn about their lives beyond the classroom. He then described the development of "Notes to Mr. G" as a tool for bringing these theories into action in the classroom through informal assessment and dialogue. Through applying these theoretical constructs, Mr. G focused on the importance of journaling as a way of accessing students' stories. He discussed accessible, relevant prompts as entry points into student writing and the idea of generating a conversation with students through "Notes to Mr. G."

As an action researcher, Mr. G's methods and data collection primarily focused on students' journals, his own daily teaching journal, and focus-group interviews that he conducted with students at the end of the school year. He attempted to triangulate the data from these different sources to address his research question: how can interactive journaling impact student-teacher connections? He coded these data and found three emergent themes: ownership of journals and journaling, student creativity, and understanding student strengths.

In describing students' ownership of journaling, he talked about multiple aspects of "Notes to Mr. G"—from the designing of the journal itself with powerful words and images of students' identities, to the writing process and the fact that students wanted to take the journals home with them and write entries that were several pages long.

He also wrote about the different journal prompts that generated the most authentic responses from students. Those prompts in which students were asked personally about an aspect of their lives outside of school seemed to generate more depth and complexity in student writing than did prompts about academic topics or school culture, for example.

Student creativity, Mr. G's second finding, went beyond the designing of journal covers and descriptive language in their writing. Mr. G. uncovered a strong connection between art and writing for some of his students. This led to options for students adding drawing to some of their journal entries, as well as further opportunities to make connections with concepts in class and with Mr. G as a person. As alluded to at the start of this chapter, the excerpt below describes some of this finding:

> Art played a huge role in creating an opportunity to spark conversations outside of what was asked in the journal prompts. An example of how art helped play an important role can be seen in the journal entries that Kaitlyn and I shared. Kaitlyn was a student who really loved to put her drawing skills on display. A moment where she and I started to develop a bond was at the end of one of her free-write responses. On October 22 she wrote, "When I grow up, I want to be a gamer. To be a Minecraft gamer to be exact . . ." In responding to her journal entry, I did not only want to acknowledge her artistic display, but also to collaborate with her to show my full investment in her creation as a teacher. In working together with her by adding drawings of my own, we were also able to discover a mutual interest: a love for video games.
>
> Stefanakis (2000) talks about the "interactive process of 'sitting beside the learner'" (p. 140). In thinking back to my own childhood as to how video games were perceived, the one thing that always stuck was the feelings of negativity my parents had towards them. In taking the time to understand that video games are an important part of Kaitlyn's life, I had also spent the time to understand what was culturally relevant to her. Often times when discussing cultural relevance, we tend to assume that we are talking about respecting and understanding the differences in ethnic background.
>
> When I talk about cultural relevance in this instance, I am referring to the cultural lines that are set from a generational standpoint. As adults, we find ourselves so caught up in what we deem as important that we begin to force our ideals upon those who are unwilling. In the same way that dominant cultures are accused of being insensitive to the beliefs and traditions of ethnic minorities, as adults we forget how to stop and ask what is important to our kids.

These aspects of student creativity heavily impacted Mr. G's analysis of the ways in which journaling helped to reveal students' strengths. He wrote about students finding their voice through writing as the school year went on and the idea that students were able to make connections to topics in class that helped him think of new ways to present lessons and interact with students.

Perhaps most lucid was the way in which "Notes to Mr. G" helped to build relationships that went beyond the normal or traditional view of student-teacher interaction in the classroom. Below is one example from Mr. G's action research:

> When I first met Sherry at the beginning of the school year she came off as an extremely shy and quiet student. While most of her classmates around her were chattering about before the start of school, Sherry would be one of the rare students who would quietly stand close to a wall, just observing the people around her. In class, it would be a struggle to get her to participate in discussions.
>
> Sherry would rarely be seen raising her hand. And although she was attentive and listening, even if she was called upon, it would be difficult to get her to verbally respond with anything more than a one or two-word answer. In speaking to some of her former teachers at the beginning of the school year, they would comment that Sherry was a "sweet and intelligent girl" and that it "took quite a while" before she would open up to them.
>
> For one journal entry, I asked the class to continue with the story of "Ned," in Remy Charlip's book *Fortunately*. In this read-aloud story, a child named Ned is met with a series of "fortunate" and "unfortunate" events that eventually leads him to showing up at his own surprise birthday party. In the students' journal responses, they were asked to expand on the original story by creating their own lists of "fortunate" and "unfortunate" events. The students were allowed the freedom to either respond in an essay format, or if they wished, to draw out their response as a comic strip with captions to explain their images.
>
> In Sherry's response, rather than staying with the character Ned, she decided to alter the story so that it would be about a girl named "Lisa." In her response, she drew beautifully detailed pictures and even changed the story by having it end with an "unfortunate" occurrence rather than a happy ending like the original story. I was impressed with the creativity that she had displayed in her comic strip. This was my response to her journal entry on August 25:
>
> "I love the way you took the story we read in class and then made an entirely new story about a girl named Lisa! Very creative; that girl was totally having a bad day! How would you have ended the story if you wanted to make it a happy ending?"
>
> From this first initial interaction that we had through "Notes to Mr. G," I was able to gather that there was much more to Sherry than the calm and quiet demeanor that she portrayed. Her willingness to modify the story and even change the format of the original story's ending revealed a glimpse of the creative individual that she truly was. My response to her journal entry was intended to encourage her to continue to show her creativity. I felt that if I could give her a sense that this writing journal was a safe space to express her ideas, that in the future she would be more forthcoming with her thoughts and ideas.
>
> Although there were signs that Sherry was receptive to the idea of expressing herself through "Notes to Mr. G," it would take several more written interactions with her before I could get her to more freely convey her thoughts. In preparation for the following journal topic, we had a discussion in the class about the concept of expectations. In introducing the topic, we discussed different sorts of expectations; those that they had for themselves, the expecta-

tions others had of them, and the struggles they experienced when trying to meet those expectations.

In Sherry's journal, she simply responded to this prompt saying "I never had one." Although her answer was short and generalized, I decided to try to elaborate on her response by writing, "I agree, it's hard to think of actual expectations that people have for you. No one ever actually says, 'Sherry, this is what I expect of you!' But I'm sure there are times when even though nobody says it, the expectations of you were either really easy or really hard to meet." —August 25.

Because Sherry was hesitant in offering her opinion, I felt that it was important to take the initiative and do what I could to elaborate further on her response; to consciously show her that I was making an effort to understand her perspective on the matter. The difficulty in getting Sherry to personally invest herself with these journal responses continued until September 7, when I asked the class to write about ways they would improve the classroom environment if they could.

In her response she stated, "I think a good classroom improvement is having more books. I think having more choices to choose from would be very helpful. I think we should have a class pet. Maybe like a hamster, a fish, or something like that. I have always wanted a puppy, but I don't think it would be the best class pet."

Up until this point, this was the first time that she had ever revealed something personal about herself. In prior journal responses, Sherry would give generic answers to a journal prompts and refuse to be more forthcoming in her comments. But in this instance, she finally opened up and revealed that she had always wanted a puppy.

Responding to her on September 9, I stated that "It's interesting that you're not the first person to mention that a class pet would be an improvement to our classroom. But why is that? Although it would be very cool to have a fish, hamster, or puppy, what about having a pet in the class do you think will make it better? To learn more about animals? Or is it to try to give the class more responsibilities?"

In stumbling across something that she was legitimately interested in, I was finally able to have an authentic interaction with her that she was truly invested in. In the next journal prompt where I asked for the class to share their thoughts about a September 11 discussion that we had, Sherry first acknowledged the prompt by saying,

"I feel like it wasn't a good idea to send the 911 message. I wonder how they came up with the idea. My thought about the people jumping off the building is sad. I can't believe the building was so hot that some people jumped off the building!" —September 11.

What was interesting was what came after her initial response. Through "Notes to Mr. G," Sherry actually began to initiate conversation with me without prompting. The interactions in this writing journal were true to what Facella, Rampino, and Shea (2005) state: "Some really good conversations have begun just by my bringing in something that the children recognize. The stories will begin! I encourage the students to talk and tell me stories about their lives. This usually opens the door for me to ask questions and keep the discussion going" (p. 213). Following her response to the 9/11 discussion, she willingly extended the conversation.

"Here are the answers to your questions. I feel like both of them are important. Having more responsibilities and learning more about them are both important. I feel like more fantasy books would help. Here is a question for you. If you heard that you are going to have a puppy, what would you name it and why?" —September 11, 2014

As we continued writing in "Notes to Mr. G," the conversations that we had swayed further away from the prompts that were being assigned, and became more individualized in terms of her interests. An authentic relationship was truly beginning to develop through the messages that we shared. In subsequent journal entries, Sherry would leave a sentence or two at the end of her response to reveal a little bit more about what was going on in her life.

On September 18, 2014, Sherry said, "By the way, I'm getting a puppy soon!!!! I'm so excited!!!" and even drew a small puppy below her journal entry. In a later journal entry, Sherry flipped to a blank page and left me a message asking me to "Attempt to draw a cartoon poodle (if you have time)" and in my following response I did include an attempt at drawing her a poodle. This eventually allowed our conversation to include her interests in drawing as well. In my later responses to her, I would set aside some time to color in the drawings that she would create for me in her journal entries.

The development of authentic relationships proved to be a common theme not only in Sherry's "Notes to Mr. G" but in the conversations that I had with many of her other classmates as well. In all of the "Notes to Mr. G" journals, before the students could open up and truly feel free to express their ideas in their writing, there was a need for me to show how invested I was in participating in these journal entries as well. My willingness to share with Sherry a story of my friend's dog Peanut, for example, sparked a whole discussion dealing with her love of dogs. But while communicating back and forth with these students, one thing that I did not factor in was how important generating handwritten responses was to the perception of personal investment in the journals.

It is clear, through Mr. G's reflections, that the journey of learning about his students through interactive journaling led to important growth for him as a teacher. The relationships he built with students provided opportunities for authentic writing about their cultural worlds. Through exhibiting students' assets and cultural wealth, the journals—and the relationships they represent—showcase a counternarrative to the deficit narrative in education.

IMPACTS IN THE CLASSROOM

The themes of ownership of journals and journaling, student creativity, and understanding student strengths were evident in Mr. G's classroom. When the authors visited Mr. G's classroom, they did not get to read students' journals, but they did have conversations with students about their perceptions of "Notes to Mr. G," what they felt that they had learned through doing the journaling, and why they learned these things.

Students had overwhelmingly positive remarks about "Notes to Mr. G" as a classroom activity. They talked about the fact that they could write about what they were feeling and not feel pressured to "get it right." Students shared comments like, "You can share your opinion on things, and you don't get graded on it. I don't get stressed about it," and "I think it builds confidence. I can be honest and not worried that I will make a mistake or that other people will read it."

Students also commented on how important it was for them to receive Mr. G's comments and get to learn about him. One student shared, "I am learning what happened in his life. Like, I am learning about experiences that he has had that I have never had. Like one time he wrote about a snowball fight . . . I thought, 'wow' I want to do that." Another student said, "I like how he tells us about his life . . . He likes rollercoasters . . . He likes broccoli." These openings for Mr. G to communicate with students in writing definitely had an impact on how they felt about the journals and stood out about things they liked.

These learnings were not unidirectional, however, as students also shared that Mr. G's responses often impacted their own thinking. For example, one student shared, "It helps me write about my perspective and think about new ideas . . . his answers make me think about things differently."

Students also expressed a sense of appreciation for and engagement in the accessibility of the journal prompts. They shared things like, "The questions can be kind of fun . . . or funny" and "I feel free to write about my opinions." The impact of this sense of freedom was shown in students' belief in themselves as writers and as thinkers. For example, some responses from students included: "It is like a test with all the right answers," "I feel like I can succeed," and "The answer is really from me." Further, as with Mr. G's analysis of his ability to dig more deeply into relationships with students via this journaling, one student stated, "I like sharing about myself and experience because I don't really show it that much. It is like my pride."

Mr. G also reflected on this sense of deepened and deepening relationships through journaling and the structures of "Notes to Mr. G." He talked about having fun with students through learning about some of their interests outside of the classroom and he learned about some of his own privileges and blind spots through reading their journals. For example, he learned about the reality that many of his students very rarely leave the city or even their neighborhood. In these ways, "Notes to Mr. G" provided opportunity for him to reflect on some of his own perceived strengths as a new, young teacher who shared aspects of a cultural background with many of his students. He reflects on these strengths in his action research:

> Learning about the students' personal interests through being totally invested in this project allowed for me to discover what was culturally relevant to them. In being able to understand the cultural lens that these students view the world from, as a teacher, that could be used as a tool to help make academic material more accessible and easier to comprehend for the students.

While he noted that the journal prompts directly related to classroom content did not necessarily produce the most authentic and deep responses from students, they did provide opportunities to draw more connections to their lived experience through writing. In this way, he was developing a sense of cultural understanding that was student generated.

Mr. G also learned an important lesson about feedback. Early in the year he was quick to collect and return journals with written feedback. As the year continued, the time required for feedback proved to be a challenge. At one point, he tried to save time by typing and then pasting his responses into students' journals. His students quickly let him know they did not like this change. For example, one student wrote back to him, "One last idea I have to improve is by when we write something to you, please write it back by hand. I think this way, it is more polite." He did change back to writing responses by hand and also realized that he needed to set realistic expectations for his students and for himself about the amount of feedback he would provide.

This approach is exactly what powerful academic work is like: deep student investment, a sense of ownership and agency, and permission to explore widely and deeply. So even as it attends to social and emotional dimensions, the journaling activity helps students experience successful work with other studies.

Overall, in a sense, "Notes to Mr. G" became a cultural activity in the classroom. It was not just about designing covers, accessible prompts, and interactive writing—it also became a journey that students and Mr. G shared. The relational aspects are documented in this chapter, and the growth of student perspectives as writers and scholars are evident alongside Mr. G's own analysis of his teaching and work with students.

IMPLICATIONS FOR SOCIALLY TRANSFORMATIVE PEDAGOGY

Given his desires for becoming a teacher, the research question he developed, his theoretical foundation, and his analysis of data, Mr. G felt that he did build stronger and deeper relationships with his students through "Notes to Mr. G." His focus on building relationships through collecting meaningful data is central to his teaching.

The genesis of the project and its continual development through the course of the year was something that Mr. G shared in with his students.

Their learning about themselves and about one another was important. As an action researcher, Mr. G shared about his own learnings as a new teacher and how vital it was for him to be completely invested in the entire process:

> Each theme was interrelated and each was necessary for the success of this project. In terms of investment, both the students and I needed to be fully bought into the idea of having a low-risk, low-anxiety space where we could get to know each other. The authenticity of the relationships that were built through this writing project depended on how much students were willing to invest into these journals, and a better understanding of what was culturally relevant to them could only be achieved through the building of authentic relationships.

He then went on to discuss the important work that he needs to do as a teacher to make content more meaningful in the short term for students so that they can draw connections to longer-term goals and learning objectives in class. This practice was reflected in the way that students engaged in and with the journal prompts:

> I also came to realize that this disconnect in communication was due to cultural differences between teacher and student at multiple levels . . . As long as the students felt that the activity they were participating in was fun, they would be more willing to engage. Teachers, in taking into consideration the long-term benefits of what they teach, struggle to get their students to sacrifice their satisfaction in the short-term, so that they may benefit in the long run. Having to learn something new is often a struggle, and because students are unwilling to experience the discomfort of learning, their priorities of having fun conflict with the teacher's goal of trying to teach.

He further wrote about ways in which culturally relevant data collection, for him, has to involve a deep desire to learn about what students are bringing with them to class each and every day. Again, this brought him back to a level of self-reflection about ways he can break down some of the barriers that exist between student and teacher. For example, he wrote: "A cultural disconnect also exists in terms of what is generationally relevant between adults and children."

This disconnect is not only important for an example like gaming, but also for issues of cultural expectations, voice, and opportunities to feel that one belongs at school. Mr. G reflected on the ways he needs to continually assess his own expectations for students and himself in a quest to remain culturally relevant.

Interactive journaling is not novel. It is a strategy that works, and, if done effectively, can encourage students to write authentically. "Notes to Mr. G" proved effective as an example of authentic, meaningful data sharing for Mr. G and his students because the aim of the journaling was centered on building relationships. There are many different ways to develop student writing in the classroom, and "Notes to Mr. G" was a deliberate attempt to make writing personal, accessible, and relational in the classroom.

It was this relational aspect of the journals that helped Mr. G achieve some of his goals as a new teacher and researcher, and also drew students into the activity. For example, one of the things they enjoyed most was learning about aspects of Mr. G's life beyond the classroom. Students' productivity as writers was evident in the abundance of written pages at the end of the year, but more importantly, their reflections on "Notes to Mr. G" reveal a deeper understanding of learning and self. In this way, the journaling was a model for connecting classroom learning to students' lived experiences.

Similarly, for Mr. G, the process of developing, enacting, and studying the impacts of "Notes to Mr. G" on connections with students proved important for his own self-reflection and growth as a teacher. He quickly realized that this activity required total commitment and investment on his part, and as a new teacher, his dedication to providing meaningful written feedback to students provided learning opportunities for him and his students. They co-created conversations in the journals, and in so doing, the journaling served as a starting point for addressing issues of power and hierarchy for students and teachers.

While Mr. G's focus as a teacher and action researcher centered on building relationships, the potential for "Notes to Mr. G" to continue to develop as a tool for him and his students to think critically about curriculum is strong. He is building foundations for awareness of student voice through writing, and providing opportunities for himself and his students to bring themselves into the classroom as living, breathing, multidimensional beings. It is this authenticity of Mr. G's approach to teaching that makes "Notes to Mr. G" an important model.

KEY IDEAS IN THIS CHAPTER

- Mr. G is a fifth-grade teacher at a public school in the Chinatown neighborhood in San Francisco. He sees his work as a new teacher as a way to be a part of—and give back to—the community.
- Mr. G sought to build relationships with students through learning as much as he could about their lives—interactive journaling was a part of this data collection.
- Mr. G's action research sought to answer the question, "How can interactive journaling impact student-teacher connections?" His findings focus on three themes: ownership of journals and journaling, student creativity, and understanding student strengths.

- Though not a novel strategy, interactive journaling, when done effectively, can encourage young people to write authentically and creatively while allowing teachers to build strong relationships with students.

Chapter Two

Reflections on Mr. G

*Humanizing Connections
through Relevant Data*

"Notes to Mr. G" marks a starting point—a first step for Mr. G as a socially transformative teacher, and the opening stage of a cyclical process of action research. The data that Mr. G continuously collects and reflects upon through interactive journaling are the foundation upon which he begins to build meaningful relationships with his students. These data involve important skills and concepts for fifth graders, and as important, they teach Mr. G and students about one other as human beings. This humanizing approach to data generation and analysis is instrumental in the study of socially transformative pedagogy.

In contrast to the culturally relevant data sought through "Notes to Mr. G," phrases like "value-added measures" and "data-driven instruction" are buzzwords in K–12 education today that denote hollow, top-down approaches to classroom data and analysis. They are the topics of countless journals, books, conferences, and educational forums. Perhaps they are most widely used by school administrators who are communicating the need for teachers to utilize instructional practices that improve the outcomes of standardized student academic achievement measures. In other words, principals want teachers to use test data to inform the instructional practices and content that they teach.

Conceptually, this makes sense—teachers need to use assessments (informal and formal) to better understand students and to teach accordingly. However, the question, "Which data counts?" is rarely asked. Teachers' voices are largely missing in debates about data because a reliance on standardized test scores empowers district and school administrators to become data czars.

Given the fact that such leaders spend little to no time with youth at school, this concept of data ownership and data-driven instruction is in dire need of interrogation.

THE PERILS OF A "VALUE-ADDED" MANTRA

From a Freirean perspective, the ways in which the predominant landscape of education thinks of data-driven instruction are dehumanizing. The current, national schooling climate calling for data-driven instruction took root in the context of the No Child Left Behind Act of 2001. The No Child Left Behind Act aimed to close the purported achievement gap, with the ultimate goal of accomplishing 100 percent competency in performance-based assessments by 2014. The primary performance-based assessments used to determine competency have reflected value-added models, measuring teacher effectiveness by projecting future student performance based on past test scores. In essence, the difference between a child's actual and projected test results is the estimated value of a student that a teacher is adding or subtracting during a school year.

The use of value added measures were made more consequential with Race to the Top (initially passed in 2012), which essentially made standardized education more punitive. Inherent in this technocratic, learn-to-earn approach to school, educators, students, communities, and schools are treated as numbers—where the bottom line has less to do with holistic growth over time and more to do with the value one might have in a market-driven society.

The pressures undergirding learning standards and standardized test scores not only led to publicly shaming teachers and releasing teachers in mass, but were also used as the premise for shutting down public schools and justifying the rise of the charter school movement. Business models of efficiency are privileged in measuring teacher effectiveness. For a time, the *Los Angeles Times* and *New York Times* were releasing data about individual teacher performance as part of this shaming process and they were doing so without explaining the context so the general public could understand the dynamics taking place in the classroom. Ultimately, evaluating data in this way tends to target novice teachers in low-performing schools. This becomes the context in which educators find themselves—their value as teachers is based on value added models of education.

Policy makers, district- and site-level administrators issue out a set of decisions, a set of funding choices, a set of policies, which are then imposed onto the people that actually have to execute those on the ground with students, and there is a clear mismatch and disconnect taking place on multiple levels. There is a cultural and racial mismatch between who is defining data, who is being asked to implement decisions based on data, and who is most impacted by those decisions. The results of these layers of mismatch are any number of problems that we see in schools and districts across the country.

TEACHER RESEARCHERS AND THE NEED FOR ACTION RESEARCH

Given the overarching idea of tests being standardized to assess all students, the instruction may be driven by data, but the data are often irrelevant to both teacher and student. There is no ownership of such data by teachers, especially for new teachers who are often seeing and administering these standardized assessments for the first time, and students simply become storage spaces for information that supposedly reflects their grade level achievement.

Data need to be presented differently in teaching. Yes, data are vital to effective teaching—all data, from a student's facial expression walking into class to his or her performance on the final essay. The generation of meaningful, relevant data then becomes the job of socially transformative teachers. And as shown in Mr. G's classroom, this task is at the heart of learning about and building relationships with students.

In the UESJ program, action research (e.g., Mertler, 2012) and youth participatory action research (YPAR) are positioned as tools for teachers and students to take an active role in reclaiming "data" as something that they generate and own in the classroom each day. The cycle of inquiry that lies at the heart of action research—one in which teachers are continually planning, implementing, assessing, and reflecting—relies on data that are meaningful to both students and teachers.

This action research process requires teachers to reclaim data as generative and humanizing building blocks upon which relationships and learning are formed. In such ways—as showcased through "Notes to Mr. G"—culturally relevant data represent the seeds of socially transformative pedagogy.

Teachers must develop a pedagogy that is addressing their students' cultural, socioemotional, and academic needs simultaneously. This is not a linear process, and these aspects of teaching are equally significant and have an impact on each other at different places in different ways. A primary contradiction that is often played out in schools is a lack of common purpose among stakeholders—students, families and guardians, teachers, and administrators.

What parents think about when they call for a more quality education for their children is often very different than what teachers and administrators think about—which is often different, even, than what students think. There is an unstated, common sense, make-believe common purpose driven by educational policy reform efforts that really shapes how teachers are pressured to understand limited forms of data, and how to move forward with using this information (Kumashiro, 2012). At key moments, however, when students really need teachers to respond to their needs, the ways teachers are trained to understand data will not help them wrap their heads around what is the appropriate approach to actually support their students.

COLLECTING MEANINGFUL DATA AND ENGAGING IN THEORY-INFORMED PRAXIS

To balance the ways in which value added measures and data-driven instruction will be imposed on new teachers, candidates in the UESJ program are taught to collect data that are useful to them as teachers by researching their own practice and connecting with their own students. The lens they use and the questions they develop to guide this research are grounded in the critical, asset-based theories that are outlined in the introductory chapter to this book.

As seen through the glimpse into Mr. G's classroom, this approach is not one-size-fits-all. It is teacher- and student-generated and it is organic. Through action research, these early career teachers conduct critical qualitative analysis to put forth teaching processes for engaging youth in urban schools through collecting culturally relevant data that begin with students' realities and ways of communicating their understanding of the world.

Being treated as intellectuals (Giroux, 1988), teacher candidates pursue their areas of research with the intent to improve their understanding of the sociocultural context in which their teaching and student learning is taking place, to inform practices serving students whose cultural realities are too often silenced in schools. Teacher candidates are encouraged to embark on this research by reflecting on their own positionality and learning as much as they possibly can about their students and their teaching context—claiming their daily interactions with students as meaningful data.

As discussed above, there is a mismatch in the perceived value of the data that schools collect on teaching and learning and the actual data that are needed to be collected by teachers to improve their practice and student learning. Data from standardized tests are not real indicators of students' abilities to learn, especially when standardized tests have been proven to be culturally biased. To combat this reality, teachers must be treated as intellectuals capable of evaluating their students' and their own growth over time, in line with the cultural and academic needs of the communities they are serving.

This practice is reinforced by recruiting students who are reflective of the communities of the students whom they seek to serve. Programmatically, UESJ recruits and admits numerous students from sociology, ethnic studies, gender studies, social psychology, and other disciplines that ground their training in socially conscious analysis. For students who do not have the racial experiences of the students that are in their classrooms, they are required to have a history of engagement in communities that reflect the demographic of the students they are going to teach, often working in community-based organizations that have served those capacities.

Further, UESJ candidates are required to study research that is focused on more effectively serving the needs of urban communities. As people who have either overcome social oppression in their own lives, or people committed to transforming social oppression, they have a vested interest in seeing historically marginalized students overcome social marginalization. Ultimately, teachers must understand their own lived experiences and their own purpose as educators as a form of data.

How does their purpose align with what they are experiencing in schools and with the students in their own classrooms? UESJ candidates determine a course of data collection based on 1) their lived experiences, 2) the analysis they developed from their informal and formal education in and out of schools, and 3) their purpose as socially just educators. They are asked questions like these: As first-year teachers in urban schools, what do you identify as the major problems, obstacles, and challenges facing students in your classroom that prevent them from engaging at the level that those who are part of the dominant culture are engaging? What types of social experiences are your students having that interfere with their learning?

First-year teachers must be able to identify the importance of these issues and understand that the academic, social, and emotional factors associated with these issues are crucial data for their classroom teaching. If what they begin to identify through such inquiry are not among the most pressing issues confronting their students, they need to reflect on why they want to conduct that research in the first place. They work to develop an analysis about the social phenomenon they would like to intervene on with their teaching.

Once they have analyzed a social and academic issue that impacts their own trajectory as a teacher and their students' lived experiences, teacher candidates develop a pedagogical framework. This theory of change, a theory of action, helps them intervene on the problem that they analyzed. Through this theory of pedagogical action, they create a pedagogy that looks to develop an aspect of their practice. This pedagogy, whether it is a curriculum, a unit, an assessment, a syllabus, or any other solution, must be informed by the theory that they created.

After designing the pedagogy, they actually implement it to collect data. They have to decide what data are important for them to collect, how that data will allow them to assess the effectiveness of their pedagogy, and what the growth areas and revisions of the project (unit, curriculum, assessment, etc.) are in order to solve the social problem with which they were intervening.

After analyzing the data that they have collected about implementing a solution to their initially identified problem, the teacher candidates have a grounded assessment to inform and analyze the usefulness, limitations, and modifications of their specific intervention.

As evidenced through "Notes to Mr. G," culturally relevant data collection was a start for Mr. G to learn about his students, mutually build relationships through written dialogue, and reflect upon his own teaching. While interactive journals in and of themselves do not represent socially transformative pedagogy, their generation of meaningful, humanizing data enhanced Mr. G's impact as a new teacher.

The content of the journal prompts, for example, may not directly interrogate the social toxins and gentrification of students' neighborhood, but the relationships that burgeon through the journal exchanges represent the possibilities for Mr. G and his students to see their classroom learning as a part of the community—a part of something larger.

The idea behind this approach to data collection is that it leads to a personal reclamation of the relational foundations of teaching. From this foundation, data are positioned as central aspects of teaching—not predetermined, static barometers for achievement. When these early-career teachers participate in this process in their future pedagogy, their practice should improve based on the study that they conducted. When they feel like that area of their practice has been solidified, then they are encouraged to partake in the same teacher action approach in other areas of their teaching that need further development. They begin by addressing what they identified as their most pressing issue, which is informed by their lived experience, formal and informal studying, and their purpose as educators.

Over time, this approach to developing their practice will improve their repertoire of theory-informed praxis—reflection and action for transformative teaching—so that they can use it to more effectively serve the needs of the students in the schools and communities that they are serving as socially just teachers.

It is from this foundation of action research as a cyclical, reflective, pedagogically generative process that teachers are also researchers. Like the portrait of Mr. G and his students above, the coming chapters will continue to explore aspects of teachers' action research projects, which serve as examples of socially transformative pedagogy in action. These examples are meant to provide insight into the processes, classroom projects, and ongoing data collection that are a part of the action research of new teachers as they transition from the UESJ teacher education program to their first years in the classroom.

The case studies in the chapters to come are very different from "Notes to Mr. G" and this focus on culturally relevant data collection. They are purposefully diverse—in their grade level, teaching style, research approach, and presentation—to show that action research is not monolithic and the application of socially transformative pedagogy means many different things, to different teachers, in different contexts.

KEY IDEAS IN THIS CHAPTER

- Value-added measures and measurements of teacher effectiveness largely target new teachers in low-performing schools and have led to the closing of public schools and the rise of the charter school movement.
- All classroom data are valuable, yet there is a cultural and racial disconnect between data-driven, decision-making processes, who is being asked to implement said decisions, and who is most impacted by those decisions.
- In an effort to generate culturally relevant and meaningful data, the authors call on practicing K–12 teachers to be action researchers in the classroom.
- Action research asks teacher-scholars to analyze their own lived experiences as well as their classroom experiences to design an intervention that improves student learning and their own teaching. Action research is theory-informed praxis.

Chapter Three

Autoethnographies with Esther

Building Community and Self-Discipline

It's 11 a.m. and Raul is just arriving. Our school day starts at 8:30 a.m. He is slowly walking up the dirt hill that leads up to our two-room school tucked away in the back corner of a junior high campus. Raul looks visibly exhausted. The bags under his eyes look heavy and purple.

I approach Raul who reeks of weed and cigarettes. I tell him I'm glad he's made it, that I'm worried, that I hadn't seen him in a few days, and he looks exhausted. I ask him, "Where have you been?"

"Around," he says. He looks distraught.

He tries to walk around me, so he walks off the trail and into the tall dried up brush. I follow him. And then Raul breaks down. As tears run down his face he crouches into the brush and puts his head between his knees. In silence we stay crouched together in the brush for some time.

Raul, his sister, her boyfriend, their baby, and his parents live in a one-bedroom apartment. Raul's dad recently got into a terrible accident that nearly killed Raul's mom, and now Raul's dad is getting deported. Raul recently started using meth. He didn't say that to me, but I could see it and the other young men have told me. Raul feels like a fuck-up. He can't protect his mother, he got kicked out of school, his family is struggling financially, and now he's spending the money he makes dishwashing on drugs.

I feel terrible. Not only because I can feel Raul's pain each time he inhales between the sobs, but because I feel deeply ill-equipped to support this young man.

ESTHER'S TEACHING CONTEXT

For her first full year of teaching, UESJ alumna Esther Flores moved back to the small city in which she was raised. When she started the school year she was twenty-three years old, eager, excited, and confident to embark on teaching. She had spent the past few years working in schools that served primarily working class students of color and had deeply learned from these experiences. She knew these young people to be incredibly intelligent, resilient, and charismatic. She felt equipped to be a critical pedagogue who would empower students using lessons that were not only culturally relevant but also critiqued the social structures that created inequity.

As a high school student, Esther's experience had been isolating. The community in which she was raised is largely white and Latinx. In her graduating class of over five hundred students, 44.5 percent were Latinx and 47.5 percent were white. Despite the fact that Latinos made up nearly half of her school, she was almost always the only student of color in her more academically rigorous courses.

But race was not the only thing she didn't have in common with her peers. Esther says, "I am the daughter of immigrants, English is not my first language, and I grew up low-middle class. Counter to the dominant narrative, I excelled in academics, not only in my K–12 education but also in college." Excelling academically was central to Esther's identity. Academic rigor and academic success were two things she valued, and like many immigrant students, she saw as central to freedom and opportunity. As a first-year teacher, Esther clung to these values of academic rigor and success while simultaneously seeking to ensure that her classroom and curriculum never felt isolating to her students.

Esther chose to teach in alternative education in an attempt to (1) avoid the comprehensive high schools in her city that hadn't changed much since she had graduated, (2) continue to work with primarily working-class student of color, and (3) position herself where she was most needed and could be most effective.

Esther cotaught in an "Opportunity Program," an alternative secondary transition school for students who were expelled, facing truancy or credit problems, were transitioning out of juvenile hall, or were not allowed to attend the comprehensive or continuation schools in the area for whatever other reason.

The program was intended to be a temporary place for youth to quickly earn credits and transition to continuation high school, independent study, or back to traditional high school or junior high. Most students, however, either remained in the program through the school year or were re-incarcerated because of probation violations.

When Esther accepted the position, she was told she would teach English and social science to high school students transitioning out of juvenile hall using project-based learning (PBL). That was not the case. She taught the same seventh-to-twelfth-grade students all subjects, all day (8:30–2:30), using a highly modified version of PBL. The school used 3–5-week units that loosely encompassed science, social science, and English. For example, in a unit titled "DNA & Me," students learned about DNA as their science component, and read about the history, ethics, and policy behind genetics for English and social science credit.

Current and previous alternative education teachers had designed the units for use at both the independent study and opportunity program. Since the units were designed with independent study students in mind, much of the work was independent work for non-special-education (SpEd) and non-English language learner high school students. Each week students could earn up to 0.5 credits in each subject. Teachers shared units and were expected to follow the same sequence. Each year a pair of teachers was expected to develop two new units.

There was nothing traditional about Esther's students, her classroom, and her school structure. There were constant flashing signs that her students were not being afforded their fundamental right to a quality education. Reflecting back on the experience, Esther says this:

> I was challenged in ways I never thought I would be. I worried constantly about my students. I felt incompetent and lost hope. Daily I felt like a horrible teacher. Sometimes I couldn't even get a student to pick up a pencil. Other times I knew that the curriculum we were offering them was not only inaccessible but also, frankly, irrelevant to their daily lives. I had to learn that it was true that it was an accomplishment that my students showed up to school, and that it was true that our education system really, truly threw some students away.

Despite all the terrible things that had happened to Esther's students, she recognized above all that they were beautiful, savvy, kind, funny, honest, sharp young people who hadn't lost hope. Like most people, they were looking for someone to see their goodness, accept them and love them. Through her daily pedagogy and more explicitly through a culturally relevant and socially transformative unit she designed and implemented, she sought to help them—and herself—find hope and simultaneously sharpen their critical lens.

ESTHER'S PERSPECTIVES ON SOCIALLY TRANSFORMATIVE PEDAGOGY

Rooted in Esther's practice as a teacher is her belief in self-determination, justice, and rigor. She is committed to these beliefs because she sees our society as "grossly unequal and thus so are educational outcomes." Esther saw these inequities as a K–12 student, read plenty about them in college, and sees them every day as an educator. However, as a K–12 student, Esther was told in both subtle and overt ways that "those" students and their culture were to blame for the outcomes. She internalized these messages about her peers.

It was not until she learned about systems of oppression and read Howard Zinn's (1980/2003) *A People's History of the United States* that she began to unlearn what she had internalized by questioning America's social structure. She continues to be enraged that she was never given the time in school to examine the oppressive policies, practices, and procedures that produced these racist and classist outcomes.

Esther often wonders, "What would be different if we'd been given an education that did not create a false binary between our culture and educational attainment? How would my life be different? How would the life of my peers be different? How might our world be different?"

Through asking these questions, Esther sees her teaching as a strategy and stance for equity; it is a pedagogy of opposition to what she had been taught. Enacting this pedagogy is not just about developing curriculum that is relevant to students; it also purposefully moves beyond static measures of academic achievement to empower students as agents in the sustenance and survival of communities.

Paris and Alim (2014) developed the term "culturally sustaining pedagogy" (CSP) to describe the work of teachers who think outside the box, often risking their own place in school organizations precisely in order to better serve their students. CSP does not just defend communities but supports their struggle for power and fulfillment. CSP stands in direct opposition to the dominant narrative, to oppression, and to American notions of individualism and meritocracy.

In the classroom, CSP is about finding ways to bring students' ways of being and ways of seeing into the classroom to examine, to problematize and affirm, to build an identity as scholars, and to open windows to other ways of being.

In a class assignment for her UESJ learning theory class, Esther wrote a "Philosophy of Teaching" letter that highlights one of the tenets of CSP: continual self-reflection and awareness of one's unfinishedness as an educator:

I know how uninviting curriculum can be when you do not see yourself represented in it. I will recognize and use the knowledge my students hold in an effort to connect their lives to the classroom. As a student whose most salient feeling in the classroom was one of alienation, I teach to build knowledge but also a sense of self and community. Through a curriculum that is culturally responsive and linguistically validating, I seek to create a humanizing space inside and beyond my classroom, to promote growth, healing, and transformation. I am aware that I am constantly in process of becoming all that I wish to be. My curriculum will always be in process and contingent upon my students' realities.

I hope that students will leave my classroom with the academic literacy skills to be successful in educational spaces and beyond. Further, I hope that students will walk away from my classroom with a greater understanding of the society in which they live and their role as active subjects within it. Students in my classroom will see history as a tool for the development of self-knowledge, perspective, and solutions. In my effort to create a classroom culture that encourages and nurtures transformational resistance among my students, I hope to create a critical, conscious and motivated student body that will work toward social justice.

Esther's experience as a student, her commitment to social justice and academic rigor, and the power of youth as agents of change are at the core of her practice of CSP.

PRACTITIONER-BASED AUTOETHNOGRAPHIES FOR SOCIALLY TRANSFORMATIVE PEDAGOGY

As a teaching credential and master's student in the UESJ program, Esther felt confident about her content knowledge, pedagogical stance, and ability to develop lessons that were rigorous and relevant. What she worried most about was establishing a classroom culture of discipline—not to control her students so they could pass tests, but to engage them in a learning process that reached beyond the classroom.

Consequently, her action research project, *In Search of My Classroom X*, centered on this topic. Esther's thesis drew heavily on K. Wayne-Yang's 2009 article, "Discipline or Punish? Some Suggestions for School Policy and Teacher Practice," in which he defines a disciplined classroom as "Classroom X" and calls on educators to engage in self-reflection to improve practice so as to become effective educators.

Yang uses the moniker "Classroom X" to define a disciplined classroom—one with high structure and high engagement. Students in Classroom X learn academic and social skills in a rigorous environment early in the year so that by the end of the year they are self-directed scholars who self-identify as trained artisans—be it writers, historians, mathematicians, and so forth. The "X" in Classroom X denotes the fact that there is no universal Classroom

X. Given that Classroom X is context-specific, there is no universal strategy for creating it, and its establishment requires an ongoing problem-posing process of practitioner-based research (Yang, 2009).

Compelled by the absence of information she had received on *how* to establish classroom discipline, her own anxieties about classroom management, and the existing disproportionate punishment of students of color that directly connects to the mass incarceration of people of color as well as the academic achievement gap, Esther sought to answer Yang's call for longitudinal practitioner autoethnographies as a means toward establishing classroom discipline.

Esther borrowed from the tradition of Freire (1998) in defining discipline as rigor, authority, and freedom in autonomy. In this sense, discipline is an approach to disrupt the disproportional punishment of students of color and also a necessary condition for self-determination and social change.

Esther's action research addressed the following two questions:

1. As a young woman of color in her first year of teaching how do I find my own "Classroom X" in the context of a large diverse urban school in San Francisco?
2. What role do caring relationships, authenticity, and purpose play in creating a disciplined classroom?

In her action research, Esther explored how a new teacher creates a disciplined classroom. More specifically, she asked this: What traits are necessary in order for a new teacher to create Classroom X, a classroom characterized by high engagement, high rigor, and transformative resistance?

This research model was inspired by Esther's acute "awareness of [her] unfinishedness" (Freire, 1998). In addition, this research can be described as critical participatory action research (CPAR), a form of PAR that is intentionally emancipatory in its aims (Kemmis, 2011). Freire (1998) among other critical education theorists agrees that "There is no such thing as teaching authority without this [professional] competence. Teachers who do not take their own education seriously, who do not study, who make little effort to keep abreast of events have no moral authority to coordinate the activities of the classroom" (p. 85).

Thus, this research approach is a positive response to the deintellectualization, assumed incompetence, and high attrition rates of new teachers. The implications of this research method empower the teacher and students to take an active role in inverting the "achievement/punishment gap" and transforming their lives. These methods embrace a holistic perspective of student development and utilize ongoing, formative assessments as a part of teaching and learning. Foremost, these methods are best because they align with the idea that students and teachers are disciplined enough to engage in self-assessment and self-determination.

Through the action research process, Esther saw clearly the benefits of continued self-reflection and sought to continue this practice as a first-year teacher. As many scholars have noted, teachers are always in the process of becoming. By engaging in praxis and critical self-reflection about her work through a longitudinal practitioner autoethnography, Esther sought to become a better teacher.

Yang (2009) says, "We need to hear from mediocre teachers struggling to become great over time" (p. 60). By drawing from her master's thesis, a longitudinal practitioner autoethnography, and analyzing her first full year of teaching where she struggled to implement culturally relevant pedagogy, Esther affirms the need for longitudinal practitioner autoethnographies as a practice toward culturally sustaining and socially transformative pedagogy.

What follows is a deeper dive into Esther's action research as means to set the stage for her first full year of teaching at an opportunity program, where she struggled to create her Classroom X while designing and implementing a culturally sustaining unit under the constraints of her alternative school and her teacher induction program. At the end, Esther reflects on the impact of writing her own practitioner autoethnography, the instructional unit and its effectiveness as CSP, her areas for growth, and lessons she learned.

ESTHER'S APPROACH TO ACTION RESEARCH

For her master's thesis, Esther engaged in a continuous, iterative approach to assessment—including classroom policies regarding consequences and behavior, curriculum, one-on-one and whole-class interventions, journals of daily interactions with students, student evaluations, and student interviews. By assessing her discipline practice holistically—and placing her own self-reflection within this approach to assessment—Esther was able make deeper conclusions about her path toward Classroom X. This autoethnographic practice will support future educators in their search for Classroom X.

Keeping in mind her research questions, she described her Classroom X through the following themes: relationships, authenticity, purpose, and identity (race, gender, and age) of teacher.

Relationships

Relationships premised on *cariño* and humanization were intentionally built to assess their role in creating discipline. An analysis of classroom data found that relationships were central to building mutual respect and a classroom community. Through the trust and investment gained by these relationships, students were receptive to engaging academically, more willing to ask for help, and less likely to disrespect their peers and the teacher.

Relationships were a key aspect to establishing a disciplined environment. This is significant because through relationships Esther was able to practice the radical inclusion and inversion of the discipline gap characteristic of Classroom X. Relationships became critical when it came to students seeing themselves as change makers. Students knew that they would have each other's backs in their collective journey toward a more humanizing world. Without these relationships, using discipline as a means for social change would be impossible.

Authenticity

Authenticity was key in building trust, getting buy in, and developing an identity as a learner. As a teacher, Esther had to reveal her vulnerability and incompleteness, thus showing her willingness to grow. She had to be honest and humble in order to be truly authentic. Educators who model authenticity help to develop in young people the ability to painfully examine themselves and their reality. Only through an authentic dissection of self and history can students begin to create a just world.

Practicing authenticity allowed Esther to demand from students a commitment to growth, self-care, and passion. Key to authenticity was risk-taking with curriculum and allowing for feedback. Asking and taking feedback was essential—students saw Esther's eagerness to learn and improve and were therefore more willing to try to do the same. Through this vulnerable practice, Esther began to develop an authority authentic to who she saw herself to be as a teacher.

Purpose

Teaching with purpose led to higher engagement, in turn reducing the need to "manage" the class. The sense of purpose that some students were able to express by the end of Esther's time with them shows that learning became a meaningful act for them. To convey this purpose, Esther sought to teach students using multiple perspectives and critical curriculum. The concepts of causality, hegemony, oppression, resistance, democracy, and the role of SWARM (straight white American rich men) were central in her teaching of US history.

Through purpose students began to see themselves as creators of knowledge and agents of change, a central piece of Classroom X. Purpose allowed Esther to commit to teaching. The purpose that she clearly articulated to herself and that she tried to continually articulate to her students nurtured her. The time she spent articulating this purpose prior to entering the classroom ensured that she knew that there would be fruits to the difficult labor of teaching. Acting upon her purpose and teaching with purpose made it so that students, too, became vehicles for social justice.

Teacher's Identities

When explaining characteristics of Classroom X, Yang (2009) emphasizes that they are contextual and made up of distinct and often indistinct facets. Identity markers particularly around age and gender were prevalent in Esther's classroom. In her search for Classroom X, identity played a distinctive role in establishing discipline. In order to find her Classroom X, it was imperative that she assess and analyze the explicit and implicit ways in which the intersection of her age (twenty-three years old), race (Chicana/Mexicana/Latina), and gender (cis woman) came to affect her path toward establishing discipline.

Esther began to see her identity as the principal barrier to establishing discipline. However, by engaging in practitioner autoethnographic writing and reflection, Esther was able to critically examine herself and build her identity as an elder and educator. This process of coming to see herself as an educator helped her understand the ways in which she can act more effectively in the classroom as a young woman of color. Practicing autoethnographic writing forced her to think critically and to act purposefully to model feminism and authority as a woman of color.

Esther's Continued Search for Classroom X: Using Culturally Sustaining Curriculum to Build Self-Discipline

Keeping in mind the themes above, Esther worked to create discipline in her new classroom when she began at the opportunity program for her first full year of teaching. She knew to keep relationships, authenticity, and purpose as central components of her everyday teaching practice while being keenly committed to developing her identity as a feminist authority figure of color. Given the structure of the opportunity program (self-contained classroom, all subjects, varied grade levels, and mandated curriculum) and the varying needs of her students, establishing discipline was more of a challenge than Esther ever could have imagined.

Building relationships was a challenge when new students came and went every few days, students regularly attended intoxicated, and Esther, as their teacher, felt terribly unprepared and unequipped to support students with their most urgent needs around their mental health, criminalization, as well as racism and classism directed at them. In this new setting—as reflected in the opening vignette to this chapter—Esther's authentic self was confused, angry, shocked, and mostly at a loss.

In many cases, Esther reverted to what she had been told to do which was content, content, content so that students would earn credit. Not only did this contradict her instincts as a teacher and the initial findings from her action research, but this narrow view of teaching also reinforced the notions of standardization and rote learning that she was committed to fighting against through CSP.

Thinking back on her first full year of teaching, Esther distinctly recalls that at one of the points in which it became most challenging, one of her superiors suggested that instead of really pushing the students to work, she should just let them do as they please as long as they didn't break rules. The supervisor advised that students should approach her if they wanted help with the worksheets and tests that were assigned.

Authenticity wasn't just a challenge for Esther. In a school setting where probation officers stopped by to check for attendance, drug test students, or meet one-on-one while peers regularly boasted about drug use, being authentic was a danger to students. Despite all of these challenges, by the end of the first semester Esther, alongside her co-teacher, had built strong relationships with the students who had been enrolled for over ten weeks. Students knew that their teachers deeply cared about them. As a community, they saw the goodness in one another.

Esther's classroom continued to struggle with purpose throughout the year. With few exceptions, most of the prescribed lessons were designed to be done individually and not at all connected to students' cultural lives. Given that lessons were designed with independent study students in mind—none of whom were special education or middle school students and most of whom were middle to upper class—these assignments were not only culturally irrelevant but also inaccessible to most of Esther's students. Purpose was missing in the classroom.

The purpose communicated to students and teachers of the opportunity program was to get students caught up on credit. Credits, credits, credits. Again, this narrow view of learning and assessment directly contrasted with Esther's vision for teaching. Rarely did the curriculum address a larger vision of self-determination and liberation.

When the opportunity came to generate and implement a unit, Esther sought to create a culturally sustaining unit that would help her build relationships with students, push her and the students to critically self-examine to be their better authentic selves, and provide purpose and meaning. The unit would have to do all that and still fall within the constraints of the teacher induction program for which Esther would have to create this unit.

This task of designing and implementing a unit would ultimately determine whether she could "pass" and continue on the process toward clearing her teacher credential while also having it be something that all of the teachers in alternative education deemed academic, accessible, independent and project-based enough to be used across all independent study and opportunity program sites.

Esther designed a four-week unit titled "Adolescent Issues." The science lessons for this unit were developed primarily by Esther's co-teacher and centered on puberty, brain development, and mental health among adolescents. Esther focused on developing the English and social science lessons around the book *We Beat the Street: How a Friendship Pact Led to Success.*

Written by one of the characters himself, the autobiographical young adult nonfiction book tells the true story of three black young men growing up in inner city Newark during the 1980s drug epidemic. The story follows the boys as they grow up, face challenges, and make mistakes. Through their support of one another alongside community and familial support, the young men ultimately achieve their goals of becoming doctors in the same community where they grew up.

The book had been chosen by teachers at Esther's teaching site because it met the criteria: it was new to all students, was right above their average reading level (sixth grade), and potentially relevant to the lives of the students in the opportunity program.

Through the unit she hoped to develop higher order literacy skills, have students understand the concept of causality and the role of history in shaping their own lives, and identify and explain the community cultural wealth (Yosso, 2005) in their community. Esther hoped that through the examples of the novel's characters, students would begin to see the positivity and possibility in their lives, things that are either painted as deficits or made invisible to them by society.

Since the book does tend to highlight the negative peer pressure, crime, and drug use in their community, Esther specifically designed additional assignments that pushed students to analyze the conditions that made the young men's neighborhoods this way, and to also identify the positivity in these young men's lives that helped them be successful.

"ADOLESCENT ISSUES" UNIT OVERVIEW

The assignments below are described to provide insight into the details of the "Adolescent Issues" unit:

- Newark Walkouts—A reading of articles on 2014 and 2015 walkouts led by youth in Newark. At the end of the reading, students must create a list of demands or requirements for all schools.
- Social and Economic Issues of the 1980s and 1990s—Reading and analysis of excerpts from a scholarly article explaining deindustrialization, ra-

cist backlash post–Civil Rights, the crack epidemic, erosion of the public sector, and the rise of mass incarceration.
- Summer Program Design—From the assignment description: Many cities and nonprofit organizations try to design programs for teens to participate in during the summer (many of them are free), but they find that teens just never seem interested in them. As a teenager yourself, pretend you are working as a consultant for the city parks and recreation division. Design a program that you think will help get teens like you involved.
- The War on Drugs—An adaptation of a guide to Frontline's "Drug Wars" (2000), created by Reggie Finlayson, designed to provide historical context for the drug epidemic taking place in the main characters' neighborhood. The reading and videos are meant to explain to students the role of the government in perpetuating the drug epidemic and accompanying violence and poverty in urban communities.
- Whose Culture Has Capital?—Excerpts from Yosso's (2005) article on community cultural wealth and an assignment for students to identify examples of community cultural wealth in the book and in their own lives.
- Wealth and Poverty in America—A four-page excerpt from Zinn's (2009) *A Young People's History of the United States* explaining Reagan's demise of the welfare program and its impact on racial wealth and poverty gaps.
- Not Another Statistic—Students read and analyze two articles that present statistics on African American men from a dominant narrative and counter narrative perspective.
- Historical Context—Brief reading explaining historical context and then a call to examine the impact of key historical events on characters' lives and students' lives.

Other assignments included a weekly reading log that students had to complete that included writing a summary, reflection, vocabulary chart, and answering analysis and thematic questions. These logs were intended to help them with the culminating English assignment of writing an autoethnographic piece on their greatest mistake and writing a letter to their future selves. Students were also exposed to guest speakers and community resources during the unit in an attempt to bridge the community with the school.

Esther developed this unit as a way to build self-discipline, create structure and investment in her classroom which for most of the year had lacked that, and as an attempt for her to have a say in the curriculum toward her Classroom X. Through the unit, Esther continued to build relationships with students as well as with the larger community and students' families. They would sit together at a table and identify community cultural wealth; in answering reading log questions that called upon personal experience, they'd share stories; through their narrative assignment, guest speakers, and other activities they worked to build the relationships necessary to thrive.

By integrating social science readings that explained the role of racism and capitalism in urban poverty as well as the drug epidemics, students sharpened their critical lenses and nurtured their purpose. By calling on students to analyze themselves and the characters that had made similar decisions as they did, they engaged in authentic conversations about the present and their hopes for the future. Students and teachers shared their greatest mistakes in narrative writing and expressed hope for the future in their letters to their future selves.

As part of her longitudinal practitioner autoethnography, Esther had to examine the hopelessness and alienation she felt that first full year of teaching, and she had to examine the relationship it did or did not have with being back in the city where schooling had been truly isolating for her while growing up.

What would it mean for her as a teacher to really connect with her students whose lived experiences were seemingly so different but at the core really similar? What would it take for them to have solidarity with one another like the characters did in the book? What power did they have to change and how could Esther maintain hope in her students, in herself as an educator, in the institution of public education, and ultimately in just change?

Developing a unit—flawed as it was—and asking these questions helped Esther truly engage in CSP and develop professionally. In a year that had been so challenging, to self-analyze as a teacher within her historical context helped Esther be hopeful, rooted in purpose, and committed to growth.

FINDING CLASSROOM X

Educators committed to building alongside young people engaged in making change must embark on their own search for Classroom X. Given the current lack of preparation that preservice teachers receive on classroom management despite the anxiety that many experience around it, this commitment to self-reflection for discipline is necessary.

In redefining discipline as a systematic and organized way to move toward justice, socially transformative teachers execute their hope and commitment to a just world. Educators must be willing to engage in the difficult practice of self-examination in order to demand the same from their students. Only through this deep self-reflection can teachers develop a truly humanizing and rigorous pedagogy.

In Esther's search for Classroom X, she found that authentic relationships rooted in purpose serve to establish discipline in the classroom. While she may not have achieved Classroom X, her longitudinal autoethnographic study allowed her to identify the ways in which she continues to move forward toward Classroom X.

The caring relationships that she built with students and that students built with one another served to increase engagement, prevent disrespectful and disruptive behavior, and most vitally encourage learning and cement trust. In the context of an education system that often makes young people feel powerless, compassionate authentic relationships can be healing and empowering for students.

Authentic teaching models teachers' abilities to learn, their struggles for growth, and the empathy that they seek to teach their students. As Diamond (2008) defines it, authentic teaching is the habit teachers practice "to learn about [themselves], to learn about the children in [their] care, to examine the possibilities that a teaching setting can provide" (p. 148).

For the teacher who seeks to be a model of discipline, competencies for authenticity include "self-awareness, knowing the relationship between feelings, thoughts and emotions, skills in personal decision making, managing feelings, and handling stress" (Stanley, 1998, p. 255). The practice of reflection ensures the development of a disciplinary strategy authentic to oneself.

Classroom X is a space where discipline is sought not for compliance but for self-determination and justice. To truly find Classroom X, educators must integrate a sense of urgency and purpose into their teaching. Students are learning not to gain academic skills but to gain the critical academic literacy skills in order to transform their lives and communities.

Through purposeful teaching and culturally sustaining curriculum, young people can acquire "the discipline and the critical consciousness required to ignite an insurrection and demand the recognition of their humanity" (Brion-Meisels et al., 2010, p. 27). This is where Esther fell short in her search for Classroom X. Without being intentional and diligent about communicating purpose through the course of the year, most students did not develop the self-discipline she sought to develop in them.

As a young woman of color, Esther found that her path toward discipline was very much affected by key aspects of her identity. Like most things in American society, gender, age, and race are inextricably linked to the ways in which people read and respond to one another. Not having reflected upon the ways that her students—who were only five to seven years younger than she was—would respond to Esther's identity challenged her.

These instances, alongside the building of discipline, were particularly challenging for Esther because she had not yet transitioned into seeing herself as an adult with authority, let alone an elder. Having never been out of school, Esther primarily saw herself as a student. This self-identification proved challenging in her path toward seeing herself as the leader and elder that teachers ought to be.

In addition, not having expected sexism and ageism in the classroom, Esther struggled to claim the righteous indignation she was very personally experiencing. In her struggle to claim her indignation, students were not held accountable, and Esther reproduced gendered and racial expectations for women of color. Only by authentically confronting and claiming her identity as an elder and feminist was she able to challenge oppression at the personal level and model for students the kind of self-righteousness she sought to develop in them.

Esther's research models for educators the imperative for *ongoing* practitioner-based assessment and research. Classroom X is not a universal classroom and, thus, Esther's search for it continues. In reflecting on her continued search for Classroom X, Esther says,

> We must be brave enough to commit to this perpetual search for the sake of our young people and for ourselves. Our institutions, be it teacher preparation programs or teacher induction programs must promote this model of pedagogical reflection. In our search for Classroom X we commit unconditionally to inclusion, rigor, and risk and, thus, provide for our young people the space to develop into a community of critical creators of new realities for themselves and for their communities.

Through this process, Esther acknowledges her own growth as a teacher. And she understands that the love and the pain that she feels for Raul—whose arrival to class opens this chapter—and so many of her students are a part of who she is as a socially transformative teacher.

KEY IDEAS IN THIS CHAPTER

- Esther, a UESJ alumna, reflects on the action research that she developed during her time in the program, which focused on her search for Classroom X, a classroom with high structure and high engagement as explained by Yang (2009). She builds on her initial research by engaging in an ongoing practitioner-based autoethnography rooted in self-reflection and self-determination.
- In her first full year of teaching at an opportunity program within alternative education, Esther continues her search for Classroom X while reflecting on the challenges she faced to develop purpose and authenticity in the classroom.
- Esther's development of an "Adolescent Issues" unit responded to the issues she and her students experienced during that academic year, and her response was to develop a culturally sustaining and socially transformative pedagogy authentic to her identity as a young woman of color.

Chapter Four

Reflections on Esther

Assessment — Authentic versus Repressive

One critical finding in examining Esther's work is her constant monitoring—her formative assessments not only of her students' progress but of her own growth as a teacher. At its best, assessment is a reflective practice for everyone in the classroom space. This chapter examines the kinds of assessments that characterize "mainstream" schooling, in sharp contrast to the rigorous and generative assessment process that Esther and other socially transformative educators pursue.

One view of our current educational system shows students entering classrooms, taking tests to measure what they are not good at, and then continuing to take test after test on these very same things. This view points to two pillars of public schooling in the United States today: an overdone emphasis on standardized evaluations and a deficit-laden approach to teaching and learning that focuses on what students supposedly cannot do.

The narrow, predetermined matrices of achievement in public education, and the testing regime behind them, have actually "dumbed down" the curriculum, stifled creativity, and pressured teachers to act only as clerks, giving test-prep lessons and administering tests. The story of Esther, and the other case studies in this book, demonstrate that the process of learning, and the possibilities of generative and expansive exploration of the world, are much richer and more meaningful in the classrooms of critical, socially transformative educators.

Esther's focus on the social and historical factors impacting her teaching context shows what is at stake for many new teachers. And, given the important research of educational scholars who help to scrutinize today's narrative surrounding educational success (e.g., Ladson-Billings, 2016), it is clear that the so-called achievement gap between White students and students of color embodies the problems of relying on standardized measures within an inequitable system (Duncan-Andrade, 2007). What is needed is a robust counter-narrative to the focus on the supposed weaknesses of urban, working class, students of color.

CONNECTING ASSESSMENT AND THE PURPOSE OF SCHOOLING

There is no doubt that assessment is an essential aspect of education. As we see in Esther's classroom, it is foundational to teaching and learning, as it represents an important part of the cycle of learning that calls for opportunities for reflection as a part of growth. However, much of the contemporary view of assessment—particularly in public education—is systematically centered on a static measure of students as they matriculate through the institution that is school.

In other words, assessment is perceived to be the mechanism through which all student learning is validated. However, Stefanakis (2000) nuances the definition of assessment:

> The educational community has to clarify two terms—*evaluation* and *assessment*—which are not equivalent terms. To evaluate is "to ascertain or fix the value of something according to a predetermined set of criteria." To assess, on the other hand, which is from the Latin *assidere*, means "to sit beside" in order to gather information. I define *assessment* specifically as an interactive process of "sitting beside the learner" to gather authentic and meaningful data for improving student learning, instructional practice, and educational options in the classroom. While evaluation is based only on interpreting students' products, assessment is based on gathering information on the teaching and learning process, learning products, and the interaction between teacher and learner. (p. 140)

As both Esther and Mr. G show, this view of assessment—sitting beside the learner—can look very different in different classrooms, but it is essential to advance the purposes of authentic and transformative schooling. Namely, student learning is a process, and the outcomes of this process cannot solely be evaluated by predetermined measures. In fact, meaningful learning necessitates making connections with prior experiences in the pursuit of unimaginable opportunities. This process involves a cycle of inquiry and learning by both teacher and student.

This relational foundation of assessment directly connects with socially transformative pedagogy and the learning enacted by students, classroom teachers, teacher educators, and researchers. Sociocultural approaches to learning value the fluid, contextual, historical, and intergenerational processes that contribute to ways in which we see the world and acquire new understandings (e.g., Nasir & Saxe, 2003; Nieto, 2002; Vygotsky, 1978).

From this perspective, all powerful learning is inherently tied to one's lived experience and much of one's learning happens in the presence of those with whom one has meaningful relationships. Experiences of teaching and learning continually highlight the importance of relationships and cultural contexts as pillars of effective learning.

Thus, meaningful assessment—as shown in Esther's application of culturally sustaining pedagogy—must value diversity and honor the cultural assets of teachers and students. Moreover, it is critical to understand that effective pedagogy must not only be "relevant," but it must also support the survival and generativity of the communities from where students come (Paris & Alim, 2014). Esther's classroom practice fights for this relevant and respectful pedagogy focused on surviving and thriving.

Building on this sociocultural foundation is an ecological systems theory that attempts to capture the importance of cultural identities and the intersectionality of cultural contexts in learning. Bronfenbrenner (1979) names five ecological systems—microsystem, mesosystem, exosystem, macrosystem, and chronosystem—in which learning occurs, ranging from an individual's biology and immediate surroundings, the microsystem, to the social and historical conditions of larger society, the chronosystem.

Bronfenbrenner's model showcases the bi-directional influence that these systems have on one another, and the fact that they exist and thrive together. Particularly for youth growing up in urban contexts and attending public schools, the importance of this approach to learning highlights the navigation between and across ecological contexts as vital for learning. Students are learning as young mathematicians and writers at school, for example, and they are also learning as sons, daughters, children of immigrants, and members of communities that have been systemically and institutionally silenced through the colonial project of schooling.

These theoretical groundings inform the critique of the current perspective of assessment as something that is "objective" and "standardized." Learning is not objective and school contexts are not standardized. Those who teach history or literature—or for that matter math and science—as settled truths, devoid of exploration, innovation, and curiosity, do violence to the disciplines and to students' identities. Thus, it is important to value the multidimensionality of student learning and envision assessment as something that is equally complex and changing. Esther does this through her deep care for and attention to students like Raul, and through her continual self-reflection and interrogation of her own teaching and teaching context.

From this perspective, the push for testing, testing, and more testing in American public education directly contradicts the goals of critical thinking, equity, and freedom that are at the core of a pedagogy that is socially transformative.

CURRENT PERSPECTIVES OF ACHIEVEMENT

During a recent conversation with a local middle school teacher of "newcomer students" to the district, the authors found themselves counting the number of days that teachers are expected to be testing students—not just proctoring state-mandated tests, but meeting state- and districtwide oral/written test requirements, administering school-based benchmark tests, fitting in grade-level proficiency tests, and setting aside time to prepare for these tests as required by the school administration. As the number moved through the teens and into the twenties and thirties, the teacher reflected that, on average, she was being expected to test her students—on items beyond her curricular involvement—once a week.

While perhaps not representative of a testing schedule for all public school teachers, the experiences of this new teacher and her immigrant students showcase the power and prominence of standardized testing in the current education system. There is little doubt that this testing regime is gaining more and more control over how academic success and achievement are framed, and there is even less doubt that these tests will go away any time soon (e.g., Duncan-Andrade, 2007; Ladson-Billings, 2016).

Educators must unite around the reality that these tests represent only one form of evaluation that reflects relatively little about a student's learning. And thus, these tests need to be treated as such: a small part of the schooling experience. Yet, when contrasted with the experiences of teachers in many of today's urban public schools, it is clear that standardized testing is colonizing classroom teaching and learning spaces (e.g., Ayers, Laura, & Ayers, 2018; Bartolome, 1994; Goodwin, 2010; Pearlstein, 2008).

As such, socially transformative pedagogy pushes against the very premise that standardized testing is the measure of academic achievement in our public schools. This point is proven by a simple question: what is your greatest academic achievement? When asking this question—to students, teachers, community leaders, faculty, friends, family, and so on—never, ever, is the response about a state-mandated standardized test from K–12 schooling.

Yet, the narrative that persists today in public education is that academic achievement is reflected in a test score. There are historical, political, and economic foundations supporting the current testing regime, and naming them showcases the ways in which students are sorted and teachers are blamed in today's educational system.

FOUNDATIONS OF THE CURRENT TESTING REGIME

American policy and corporate forces in education argue that the market will be the leading model for improving education and that test scores will be the metric that will drive this business model of reform. Testing has been a convenient hammer in the hands of these forces. But it has unleashed a forceful opposition from parents and communities as well. The Opt-Out Movement—parents electing to have their children skip the tests, stay home, or sit in the auditorium during test time—speaks to a deep discomfort with and mistrust of the dominant testing regimen. One of the worst things about the testing system—and parents and teachers witness this up close—is that it labels very young kids as losers and winners.

That is a tragedy for all of them, and over time it becomes a catastrophe for the larger society. Many families and entire communities have concluded that the tests are expensive and disruptive but have no authentic educational benefit, and many are becoming more sophisticated in analyzing the relative value of high-stakes standardized testing. People who make policy about children and schools seem pretty sure that there is a uniformity in children that can be discerned on a test. They tend to talk about "the third grader" or "the third-grade level" as if third graders were a thing—the same or similar—or as if there were a platonic ideal of "third grader." But the real world is much more messy and complex.

Testing, and especially high-stakes standardized testing as a central aspect of schooling, is a relatively recent phenomenon, and its history is enlightening if not particularly beneficent. Similar to the founding of American public schools, testing is not immune from social, political, and economic factors. The testing movement began in earnest in the early twentieth century and rapidly expanded, due in part to an unbounded faith that modern science and measurement in all areas were the keys to progress and prosperity.

Testing also drew on a belief in the "science of eugenics"—the movement to sort humanity into complex systems of superior and inferior races and ethnicities. During World War I, IQ tests were widely administered to soldiers in an attempt to discover who should be elevated to the officer corps. The writer and social commentator Walter Lippmann (1922) said at the time that the tests were a form of "quackery in a field that breeds quacks like rabbits."

The SAT tests were a close cousin of the IQs, and their inventor, Carl Brigham, who never intended them to be used beyond counseling and advising, later denounced them as misused and misleading. He also pointed out that the scores were not neutral or particularly useful since they measured "schooling, family background, familiarity with English, and everything else, relevant and irrelevant."

How a particular student will do on a standardized test is correlated strongly with how that student did on the first test they ever took, and the score on that first test correlates most strongly with family income and parents' level of education. So, test results are first and foremost a measure of zip code and a test of class background, and therefore a kind of massive fraud that asks everyone to act as if they "earned" the score in an objective, context-free world. The students most harmed by high-stakes standardized tests are the least standard among us.

Rather than exploring the knotty problem of what constitutes an education of value, or what society collectively thinks the wild diversity of educated persons ought to look like, educators are told to bow low to the test and say, in effect, an educated person tests well, and we can line up educated folks, best to worst, on a linear scale. And since the testing machine can test only specific, relatively narrow things, those constricted and testable things become glorified as the things-most-needful, the markers of value in education. This process is an upside-down world that privileges banal thinking—and in the context of public schooling in the United States, thinking that is based on white, middle class norms.

WHAT DO THESE TESTS REALLY MEASURE?

Albert Einstein famously noted that not everything that can be counted counts, and not everything that counts can be counted. Think about it: how does one create a test for kindness or compassion? Kindness can be seen, practiced, and experienced, but how—and why—would one test for it? There are so many other positive qualities and powerful dispositions that count, but are not counted in school: love, initiative, curiosity, joy, justice, commitment, effort, interest, engagement, awareness, imagination, connectedness, happiness, sense of humor, relevance, friendship, gentleness, honesty, self-confidence, respect for others, and so much more.

The expensive run-away testing project could be replaced immediately by simply lining the kids up in the schoolyard from richest to poorest, and sorting them out from there, but without the false cover of objectivity offered by those high-priced tests. Further, no matter what students learn, how or what their teachers teach, or how difficult or simple a norm-referenced test is, precisely 10 percent of kids will score in the top 10 percent, and exactly half of the kids will fall below the median—not because a kid is weak or a teacher terrible, but because of the definition of median. As Professor Wayne Au has argued, "If all the students passed the test . . . that test would immediately judge an invalid metric, and any measure of students which mandates the failure of students is an invalid measure" (Hagopian, 2014).

Twenty years ago, the College Board, who owns the SATs, acknowledged that the tests had little to do with "aptitude" and dropped that word from its title, changing the name to the Scholastic *Achievement* Test. That wasn't quite right either, and so the name was changed again—it's now simply the SAT. Elizabeth Kolbert (2014) pointed out that "the letters 'SAT' stand for nothing more (or less) than SATs. As the Lord put it to Moses, 'I am that I am.'" In looking more deeply, studying for and taking the tests herself, Kolbert concluded, "As befits an exam named for itself, the SAT measures those skills—and really only those skills—necessary for the SATs."

The "testocrats," as Jesse Hagopian (2014) calls them, are the test and textbook publishers who profit extravagantly from the national obsession, but also the corporate reformers and investors who push an agenda of hyper-competition and privatization of public education in direct opposition to cooperation, collaboration, critical thought, and the expansion of the public space. Hagopian compares American testocracy to any run-of-the-mill theocracy: "a deity—in this case the exalted norm-referenced bubble exam—is officially recognized as the civil ruler of education whose policy is governed by officials that regard test results as divine." He goes on: "The testocratic elite are committed to reducing the intellectual and emotional process of teaching and learning to a single number—a score they subsequently use to sacrifice education on the altar devoted to high-stakes testing by denying students promotion or graduation, firing teachers, converting schools into privatized charters, or closing schools altogether." Hagopian bristles at the idea of "data-driven reform"; he argues for schools and classrooms that are student-driven and data-informed.

EDUCATIONAL RESEARCH AND THE OMNIPRESENCE OF THE "ACHIEVEMENT GAP"

Vast numbers of the thousands of researchers in the American Educational Research Association are "working on" the achievement gap constructed by the testing game. Researchers wring their hands, try new studies, create brilliant models, but never seem to wrestle the gap monster to its knees. If educators simply declared the gap over, all those researchers would be out of a job, destroying what's become the achievement-gap-industrial-complex.

The most honest and effective way to deal with the achievement gap is to acknowledge that it is the product of structural failures and just declare that it is a nonproblem, a problem constructed by those in power to inscribe the very elements of their defined privilege. The problem in education should be redefined as engagement, community needs, school resources, student agency, genuine inquiry in curriculum, and the full development of free people. Indeed, John Dewey (1910) advised this:

> Old ideas give way slowly, for they are more than abstract logical forms and categories. They are habits, predispositions, deeply ingrained attitudes of aversion and preference. Moreover, the conviction persists—though history shows it to be a hallucination—that all the questions that the human mind has asked are questions that can be answered in terms of the alternative that the questions themselves present. But in fact intellectual progress usually occurs through sheer abandonment of questions together with both the alternatives they assume, an abandonment that results from their decreasing vitalism and a change of urgent interest. We do not solve them; we get over them. Old questions are solved by disappearing, evaporating, while new questions corresponding to the changed attitude of endeavor and preference take place. (p. 19)

In the best of possible worlds, schools would focus on the educational and social experiences that matter and would dispense with standardized testing altogether. Educators would stop asking the question about the "achievement gap" and would instead address the far more aptly named education debt (Ladson-Billings, 2006).

In the 1990s, a mandate for strict "accountability" and higher test scores swept the nation and seemingly overnight standardized test scores were being held up as the new—and sole—measure of progress for students and schools. Simultaneously, a strict, structured, and much more prescriptive curriculum—narrowed to little more than reading and math—slipped into place. In many places the tests became the curriculum, and the impact on both students and classroom teachers was palpable. For students, it meant markedly less time to think, reflect, or participate in the arts, and dramatically more time on test preparation. For teachers, it meant reduced autonomy, increased stress levels, and decreased job satisfaction.

THE DELETERIOUS EFFECTS OF NARROW METRICS AND HIGH CONSEQUENCES

One of the clearest objections to the collective metric madness is that the weight placed on certain measures, combined with the huge consequences—high stakes—makes gaming the system inevitable. Put simply, announcing a policy with significant rewards and punishments tied to a specific measure—a measure meant to stand for an entire universe of interest—will result in people working exclusively on that designated measure to the detriment of larger and more comprehensive goals.

The following examples showcase ways in which outcomes can come to outweigh purpose. First, Urban Prep High School in Chicago built a reputation as a good school because it sent 100 percent of its graduates to college while covering up a massive push-out rate and a suspect list of what counts as "college." Second, Lutheran Hospital worked feverishly to keep patients alive for thirty-one days after surgery—often with machines doing the heavy lifting—to beat by a day Medicare's survival metric. Third, Chicago became a "safer" city when the police department removed from the homicide totals "justifiable homicide." And bureaucrats in Russia lowered the rate of traffic fatalities by reporting only deaths that occurred within five days of an accident; and on and on.

And to further display the insidiousness of ways in which the hustle avoids facing reality: *Newsweek* offers an annual list of the "best high schools" in the country. Their rating system comprises six variables: on-time graduation rate (25 percent), college acceptance rate (25 percent), A.P. and I.B. tests per student (25 percent), average SAT and ACT score (10 percent), average A.P and I.B. score (10 percent), and A.P. and I.B. courses per student (5 percent). This sounds like science—fair and objective, all neatly arranged with engineered precision. Yet here, as elsewhere, a lot depends on how one weighs the variables—40 percent of the data relies on A.P. data, and a school that doesn't offer A.P. will never make the grade, even though many excellent schools reject those classes as a waste of resources and time.

And a close look at the schools reveals a lot—of the top fifty schools, for example, 37 have selective admissions, and among the open enrollment public schools are Bronxville, New York (number 40) with a median household income of $166,000, and Jericho, New York (number 41) with a median of $128,000—compared to $54,000 for New York state as a whole. At one charter school in Arizona, the school population is 41 percent Asian in a state with 2.8 percent Asian residents, and 2 percent Hispanic in a state with 33 percent Hispanic people. The lesson is clear: to make a "best school," bring in the "best kids" and don't let the "unbest" near the place.

The previous examples look at those who distort their work to show success according to a narrow metric. Clear evidence of the corrupting influence of testing is that gaming the system, fudging and cheating, is now inevitable because of the emphasis placed on measures (testing) combined with the huge consequences (high stakes). And this is because of a simple principle that is well known in business, economics, social research, and science, but apparently not known in the field of education: a performance metric is only useful as a performance metric as long as it isn't used as a performance metric.

People will set about working exclusively on that one designated measure and ignore the larger universe of interest. So, for example, Urban Prep school in New York built a reputation as a good school (the universe) because it sent 100 percent of its graduates to college (the performance metric) while covering up a massive push-out rate and a suspect list of what counts as college.

This phenomenon explains why cheating scandals on student standardized tests have become ubiquitous—from Seattle to San Diego, from Lake Tahoe to Lake Forest. So the Department of Education is barking up the wrong tree by hiring former FBI director to secure the tests "at all costs." Moreover, the testing machine can test only specific things, and those certain testable things then become glorified as the golden things. The tail is wagging the dog.

If one believes market models and competition are the best way to measure and improve education, if one expects schools to mimic the capitalist marketplace, then one would have the very practices that characterize corporate life in America, and that means cheating. After all, every corporate annual report cooks the books, every engagement at the marketplace involves deception and distortion of the truth.

We are finding across the country that educators, under tremendous pressure from state authorities and administrators, are cheating on the tests—erasing wrong answers and filling in correct answers on hundreds of answer sheets. Even when there has not been overt cheating, such a system encourages corruption and undermines teacher collaboration (Berliner & Glass, 2014).

One of the most spectacular cases of such cheating was in Atlanta, Georgia, where eleven educators went to prison, charged with criminal conspiracy—a law designed to go after mobsters. Their crime? Changing test scores under pressure from school superintendent Beverly Hall, who was on her way to winning awards for record improvement in student test scores. The entire district had created a "culture of fear, intimidation, and retaliation" according to Richard Rothstein (2015) as district officials themselves were facing "fear, intimidation, and retaliation" from the federal government.

Rothstein adds that "Certainly, educators can refuse to cheat, and take the fall for unavoidable failure in other ways: they can see their schools closed, their colleagues fired, their students' confidence and love of learning destroyed. That would have been the legal thing to do but not necessarily the ethical thing to do." And similar cheating has been uncovered in Baltimore, Houston, Toledo, El Paso, Philadelphia, while even in Washington, DC, where Michelle Rhee claimed to have made great advances, circumstantial evidence points to success through cheating.

While bankers who are caught cheating for billions of dollars or car manufacturers who create software to deceive smog monitoring devices do not go to prison, the teachers in the Atlanta scandal were led off in chains. The optics in this case say a thousand words about the blame placed on teachers through all of this and the antiteacher narrative that has gripped the public discussion. For example, Rachel Aviv in *The New Yorker* (2014) captures in excruciating detail the agonies the teachers faced in trying to protect their students and keep their schools open in the neoliberal test and punish regime.

As Monte Neill of FairTest points out, the testing hysteria troubles teachers because it narrows the curriculum and is no use as a practical guide to teaching as it hurts kids and creates a rotten environment for learning. It also masks the real problems we have in our schools, which is, as one could expect, a reflection of real problems in the larger society: racism, entrenched poverty, inequality, brutal class distinctions.

The Department of Education (DOE) acknowledges that tests don't reveal everything that's important about a child and that they're consistently used for purposes for which they were not designed. Nevertheless, the DOE is now in the business of making tests more efficient and more intense by handing them over to private firms such as Pearson to turn a profit. And they pledge absolute fealty to the underlying ethos of metric madness: intense competition and individualism, privatization of the public sphere and tying teachers' fates to kids' test scores.

WHAT CAN TEACHERS DO?

While the forces behind the current testing regime in the US public education system are strong, the main people involved are not classroom teachers. In fact, many of the legislators, policy makers, and researchers driving the movement spend little to no time with youth in classrooms (and, incidentally, may not even send their children to public schools). While the absence of teachers' voices in educational policy making is a travesty, the reality is that teachers are doing the day-to-day work that really makes a difference in students' lives.

Therefore, critical, socially transformative teaching is a far more powerful force than the current testing regime—and for that matter, any educational policy. Teachers who build relationships and engage students in meaningful, generative, and critical thinking always have been and always will be the heart and soul of classroom learning. Depending on the policy environment they are working on, such powerful teaching will be more or less honored, or more or less subversive and driven underground.

From this perspective, Esther's classroom stands out and reflects one of the distinctions made earlier in this chapter—the difference between assessment and evaluation. The evaluation of students by standardized tests of predetermined, normed outcomes is a reality in the educational system today that will continue to sort students and teachers through a monolithic perception of academic achievement. Given this reality, teachers want all students to pass these tests. Further, teacher educators know that teachers are also evaluated by these tests, and as state employees, their jobs can sometimes depend on students' test scores. However, Esther refuses to reduce her classroom—and her students' lives—to a narrow testing metric. She deliberately assesses her students' and her own learning as a part of her search for Classroom X. This iterative, humanizing process lies at the heart of her approach to culturally sustaining pedagogy.

As a model, Esther's teaching reveals the importance of—and possibilities for—assessment being a cornerstone of effective teaching that encourages students to engage meaningfully in reciprocal, relational classroom learning that is directly connected to their lives outside of school. When such learning occurs, passing standardized tests is a byproduct, not an end goal. And, paradoxically, students who engage in powerful educational experiences do better in these tests than those stuck in boring, test-prep regimes.

Further, Esther shows that deep, honest, critical self-reflection is a hallmark of effective assessment. Through the interrogation of her own experiences—as a student, as a new teacher, and as a woman of color—Esther places herself alongside her students in the search for Classroom X. Her focus is not on classroom discipline as a mechanism for control, but rather her quest is for the creation of a socially transformative space in which her own and her students' cultural identities are fostered and an important part of classroom learning.

Esther's classroom—and her opening reflection about Raul—shows how personal and political teaching is. And it shows how humbling the process of authentic assessment—sitting alongside students—can be. As she and Raul sit beside one another they learn about themselves and they learn about each other. The importance of relationships cannot be overstated. As such, assessment is not a solitary, individualistic pursuit: it must be generative, meaningful, and reflective of students' and teachers' lived experiences. Like the foundations of contemporary learning theories presented earlier, it must foster and harness the fluidity and multidimensionality of culture to support meaningful learning in a classroom ecosystem.

The best, most powerful learning experiences that students and teachers have are those that cannot be anticipated. For children and youth in US public schools, such experiences are being blocked by a system fixated on predetermined, static measures of achievement. Esther shows how teachers can fight back against this pursuit in schools by engaging in action research, critical self-reflection, and a vision of assessment as something that is a part of their own and their students' learning.

KEY IDEAS IN THIS CHAPTER

- Narrow definitions of assessment create an educational context in which standardized testing is perceived as the only tool through which student

learning is validated. This chapter proposes expanding the dominant understanding and purpose of assessment to include the cycle of inquiry and learning.
- Looking at the history of standardized testing in the United States shows that testing has become more a measure of a student's class and family background, and less a measure of a student's academic ability and potential.
- Within a neoliberal approach to education, testing has become a convenient metric of achievement to sustain a business model of educational reform, but community opposition as evidenced by forces like the Opt-Out Movement show that these tests have long lost their initial purpose.
- Socially transformative educators must use assessment as a tool for self-reflection while humanizing their students' lives and experiences.

Chapter Five

Reading the World and the Word with Sharim and Cam

The Power of Performance Poetry

As soon as they open the door to W2, students are overwhelmed by a strong gust of hot air. It's mid-April and close to ninety degrees outside, but the bright yellow, non-air-conditioned and windowless room feels much hotter. Inside, thirty eleventh and twelfth grade students are sitting with partners, writing and talking.

Aside from the way some of them are dripping with sweat, students are seemingly unfazed by the heat as they continue their first practice session to prepare for the culmination of this unit: a poetic performance. As they practice, students reflect a clear level of comfort with one another, often stopping to tell one another to make eye contact and enunciate a word more clearly, or to simply praise their poetic strategies.

This classroom culture is largely a result of the fact that this is their third year in English class together where a collectively caring space, explained more in the following chapter, was cultivated. The school, which is 100 percent students of color, has struggled with high teacher turnover, and has agreed to let their teacher, Sharim, loop with this group of students for their four years of high school. For their junior and senior years, Cam has agreed to co-teach the class.

Cam is a professor in the Urban Education and Social Justice (UESJ) program of which Sharim is an alumna and, most recently, an adjunct professor. Their pedagogical frameworks are largely informed by their own overwhelmingly negative K–12 schooling experiences. For them, schools were disconnected from their lived experiences, silenced their voice, and dehumanized them. The consequences of this type of schooling were dire for both of them, causing them to disengage from formal education and utilize maladaptive coping mechanisms (Kohl, 1994) to deal with some of the stressors that school had left unaddressed.

Ultimately, both of them turned to teaching in hopes of being the type of teacher that they never had. Doing so has meant immersing themselves in social justice education research that informs how they attempt to create classrooms that honor the experiences of students, especially those who have been the most marginalized. Based on their similar beliefs about pedagogy, practice, and the role of education, they decided that both the teachers and the students would learn in the process of co-teaching a high school class. This case study illustrates one of Sharim and Cam's curricular units that was built upon Sharim's action research project as a UESJ student.

CURRICULUM DESIGN

As the curricular unit analyzed throughout this chapter, the "Word and the World" was intended to create the conditions for young people to understand the relationship between words, their world, and their lived experiences. Sharim and Cam's hope was that through the texts analyzed in this unit, students would be able to see the power of words, thus understanding that "power is the ability to define phenomenon and make it act in a desired manner" (Newton, 1971, p. 271). The concept of critically relevant pedagogy, unpacked more in the discussion to follow, relates to this curriculum design.

The four assignments (all assignments aligned with California and Common Core standard) for the unit included the following:

1. A timed ideological critique on the film *Slam* (Levin, 1998)
2. A literary analysis of two poems

    a. Organization:

    - Introduction (Discuss the power and significance of language by drawing on the two foundational texts for the unit)
    - Analysis of poem #1
    - Analysis of poem #2
    - Similarities and differences in poetic theme and techniques
    - Conclusion and implications

3. Two poems
4. A 5–7 minute performance of their poem, with Q&A

In order to complete these assignments, Sharim and Cam organized the unit around two foundational texts to be analyzed by the entire class: Paulo Freire and Donaldo Macedo's (1987) "Reading the Word and the World" and Marc Levin's (1998) film *Slam*. By beginning with Freire and Macedo, students were introduced to a theoretical framing of language and its relationship to power. Embedded in this ideological understanding is the argument that the ability to read and speak on one's material conditions is in fact a form of literacy often disregarded by school settings. This ideology is referred to as a critically caring literacy pedagogy in the next chapter.

By reading this text concurrently with analyzing Marc Levin's (1998) film *Slam*, students were able to see and apply Freire and Macedo's argument through the ways in which the protagonist Raymond Joshua (poet/actor Saul Williams) uses poetry and rap to make sense of his experiences living in Southeast Washington DC, and then as someone imprisoned under felony charges for being caught with a minimal amount of marijuana.

Lauren Bell (actress/poet Sonja Sohn), who becomes Joshua's romantic interest, encourages him to use his performative and literary talents as a way of coping with, navigating, and healing from the harm of being unjustly imprisoned in inhumane conditions. Sharim and Cam selected the film to reflect the historicity of black literary tradition vis-à-vis the black arts movement (BAM), as it was important for the teachers to both honor and highlight the literary legacy in communities of color. The major question for students to analyze throughout the film was this: How do the main characters use their words to make sense of and change their world?

In analyzing the film through an understanding of BAM and an analysis of Freire and Macedo's (1987) conceptualization of literacy, students were able to see the significance of literature, and poetry specifically, as well as begin to identify and analyze literary techniques and purposes. By watching both Ray Joshua and Lauren Bell write and perform their poetry as a way of releasing indignation, critiquing systems, and healing self, students were able to begin understanding their emerging role as poets and performers. One student shared this:

> Language is something that is supposed to be owned by us, since we use the words to connect them with our reality. Using your words consciously gives you power, it gives you the power to be able to name all of the injustices that surround you and being able to communicate that to others that don't have the ability to see their world cautiously.

Through this unit, students grew to see the power that words had to name and explain the experiences in their world.

To continue growing literary analysis skills, Sharim and Cam strategically grouped students to begin working on their second assignment: an analysis of two poems. The poems covered various topics, including: loss of land, struggle with identity, toxic masculinity, exploitation of women, and queer love. Some of the poems students chose included the following:

- "In Response to a Brother's Question About What He Should Do When His Best Friend Beats His Woman" by Asha Bandele
- "Self-Guamination" by Ryan Leon Guerrero and Willa Wai
- "To live in the Borderlands means you" by Gloria Anzaldúa
- "Your Revolution" by Sarah Jones
- "10 Things I Want to Say to a Black Woman" by Joshua Bennett
- "Immigrants in Our Own Land" by Jimmy Santiago Baca
- "Kaulana Na Pua" by Jamaica Osorio
- "Ego Trippin" by Nikki Giovanni
- "Motives and Thoughts" by Lauryn Hill
- "Loose Woman" by Sandra Cisneros
- "Duality Duel" by Daniel Beats
- "For Women who are Difficult to Love" by Warsan Shire
- "Dear Ex Lover" by Jasmine Mans

Through this analytical writing process, students were able to explore and understand the function of poetry as a processing tool. Another student wrote this:

> As described by Zora Neale Hurston, "If you are silent about your pain, they'll kill you and say you enjoyed it." In both poems, the poets challenge the system and the oppressors by speaking about their experiences. They name their world, and in order to change it they use their words in the form of poetry. Rather than them using and allowing the dominant narrative of the oppressor to control the conversation about their experiences, they used poetry as a counternarrative to *honor their humanity.*

The above excerpt of literary analysis illustrates young people's understanding of the poetic writing process as intrinsically tied to the process of becoming more fully human. Additionally, this analysis reflects the ideological paradigms and vocabulary taught throughout the rest of the semester and school year (i.e., systemic oppression, oppressor/oppressed, dominant/counter narrative). In this way, students are prepared with both the lexicon and skill to critically analyze their conditions, creating a strong foundation for young people to understand the power of giving words and voice to their thoughts and experiences. The following chapter features more discussion about students' capacity for sociocritical literacy.

TOWARD BECOMING MORE FULLY HUMAN

The following poems were selected from an array of beautifully composed and powerfully performed poetry from thirty students. While the poetry composed by all of the students reflected a clear poetic skill, refined through purposeful editing and practicing, only three will be shared. The three poems below were chosen because they do more than just illustrate profound poetic technique and critical thinking; they serve to disrupt the mind/body split that renders emotions insignificant.

In sharing their inner turmoil, some of their most private experiences, or political ideologies, these students create a space where students' own humanity is shared and reflected back to them. The following poems and the responses to the sharing of these poems serve to indicate the power of poetry as a tool for humanization, healing, and empathy. The first poem, performed by Alex, borrowed format and organization from Lauren Bell's performance in the film *Slam*.

If I Were to Fall

If I were half an inch from the edge i wouldn't be afraid to fall
to let go myself let my body be free.
Free like my brother wishes to be
but "chooses" to be locked behind bars,
the bars that apparently define who we are
what they think of us to be
If i were I were half an inch from the edge I wouldn't be afraid to fall
to let myself go let my body be free
free like i want my people to be but instead we are dehumanized
Traumatized by the fear they bring to us
oppressed because that's all we were ever taught to be
But one day my people will be free
They say segregation is a thing of the past but is it really?
Cause all I see in my community are the poor ass Black and Mexicans trying to make ends
meet tired from the necks straight down to the feet
see if i were half an inch from the edge i wouldn't be afraid to fall
to let myself go and let my body be free.
I look back on myself and every inch of me depending on education
like my surroundings depending on their crackpipe
thinking that magically it'll open the secret door to a better life
education is my crack you can call me a muthafuckin addict.
And the secret door will soon be open and let my imagination run free,
free like what was once promised to us when our people were colonized,
free like those the color of my paper,
free like i'm supposed to be
but what is free?
One day my people will be free

In this poem, Alex demonstrates a layered understanding of systemic power relations, making explicit reference to institutional oppression and interpersonal oppression through the line "Free like my brother wishes to be/ but 'chooses' to be locked behind bars/ the bars that apparently define who we are/ what they think of us to be." In making the decision to put quotes around the word chooses, Alex signifies a knowledge of systemic incarceration and the racist ideologies that inform the mass incarceration of people of color vis-a-vis "what they think of us to be."

Alex also reflects a mastery of rigorous vocabulary taught earlier in the year, namely in her use of "dehumanization" and "oppression." Her sociocritical literacy about oppression is then evident in her incorporation of "blacks and Mexicans." As a Latina, Alex recognizes that similar experiences among people of color in her community are caused by systematic oppression. To understand the significance of this poetic performance, it is important to contextualize this poem in relationship to Alex's trajectory as a student.

When Alex first joined this class, she had less than a 1.0 grade point average (GPA) and articulated that she found school both unnecessary and at odds with her experiences. She would often refuse to participate in assignments. It is for this reason, alongside the power of her simile, that the rest of the class erupts in cheer when she reaches the end of her fourth stanza, reciting "education is my crack you can call me a muthafuckin addict." This line demarcated a clear transformation in Alex's thinking about both herself and her schooling.

Perhaps most powerful is Alex's willingness to analyze oppression by sharing her own experiences and those of her family. When Alex first joined the class, she was remiss to confide personal experiences with anybody other than the teacher. While subtle, it is notable that she begins the poem by sharing the incarceration of her brother. Upon finishing the poem, Sharim and Cam asked Alex her motivation for the poem, and she begins sharing how long it has been since she has seen her brother, going further to share that she wishes her brother comprehended his incarceration and institutional oppression in the way that she does.

As Alex shares, she cries. Across the room, several other students with incarcerated family members cry as well. The people to the sides of them offer tissues or rub their shoulders as she courageously continues. Through sharing aloud and with others, Alex has begun an important step in the healing process, making space for the full spectrum of her human experiences—ones that she happens to share with many others in the room. In articulating her experiences through this poetic performance, she allows for other members of her community to also feel seen and heard.

The profound impact of empathetic spaces is seen later when another student, Eric, reads aloud his poem, "The Heat of Being Straight."

The Heat of Being Straight

I am a pair of blue jeans
Straight fit is the style
I was bought this way
No trades made
Been tried on a few times
And I like what I see
I think this is the style
Just right for me
I've been put in the closet
not cared for in a special way
Thrown in with the rest of the jeans
Waiting to be selected for another day
In the closet it was cold, lonely
in the presence of other clothes
All different sorts
Shirts, drawers, socks, and pants
Today was the day to come and be worn
but first i must be ironed
Placed on high board
Laid flat and made straight
Get the starch ready,
Take off the cap
And spray
The iron set on the highest heat
Time to get pressed
From the front to the back
When the iron meets me
It sticks, it slides, and steams
And when lifted up
I'm straight
Only took 16 minutes.

This poem is particularly important because it highlights the internal conflict that Eric experiences, particularly as it pertains to his sexual orientation and identification. Prior to this moment, Eric had never discussed—publicly or privately—his sexual orientation with anyone. As a Black boy raised in a conservative, religious household, Eric felt that this conflict was one he was not permitted to have, explore, or discuss. As he suggests in the poem, his sexual orientation was something to remain in the closet, and to be ironed out and hidden once in the public sphere. In both places, however, Eric remained uncomfortable and untrue to himself.

This feeling is important to note, because as previously mentioned, Eric had been in Sharim and Cam's classroom for three years, meaning that until this poetry unit, the classroom space had been one in which he also felt that he had to hide. Whether because of timing or the curricular unit at hand, this poetry unit became the opportune moment for Eric to be publicly honest with himself.

Eric's metaphor of a pair of jeans is poignant because like the commonality of blue jeans, it reflects his desire to simply fit in and remain unnoticed. In addition, his explanation of the different ways pants can be worn and molded illustrates the malleability of his persona, which as a young man, he is still trying to figure out. His last line, "it only took 16 minutes," highlights the day-to-day labor of having to prepare himself for a world he has yet to figure out how to navigate and live in authentically.

Despite the metaphor of the closet, this poem served less as a "coming out of the closet" moment and more of a sharing of the messiness of it all, of the turmoil that was weighing on his spirit. Eric's poem reveals his own fluid reading of his world as it relates to his identities.

Similarly, the comments and responses to Eric's poem reflected a deep level of love and empathy. The comments focused on affirming their love and support for Eric regardless of what he decided. Classmates applauded his courage, and for two students, they reflected feeling a similar sense of uncertainty in their own identities. This performance highlighted the potential power of poetry as a tool for saying the things you cannot say in everyday life, the things you "swallow day-to-day and attempt to make your own until you sicken and die of them" (Lorde, 1984, p. 41).

IMPLICATIONS

After all of the students had performed their individual poems, two of the girls in the class, who happened to be twins, asked if they could present a poem to the class together. The poem had been inspired by hearing other people's poems in the class and was written and performed in addition to their individual poems.

> As black womyn
> we are treated less than what we are
> We are kidnapped queens
> from our wide hips
> to our plump lips
> excluded from a
> patriarchal society that doesn't accept our kinky tresses
> we are lost
> lost souls that cannot find our way out through the dark
> we are black
> black women who can't even speak our minds without being called a ratchet bitch.
> we are mad
> two mad black womyn
> who are fed bottles after bottles of
> empty promises and sharp lies

cutting throats
blood spilling down bruised bodies covering her beauty.
Tampered beauty (together)
broken down bit by bit forced to be what
"HE"
wants us to be
but we are strong
strong enough to hold the weight of hate on our backs
and still be able to stand tall
nobody ever ask how it feels to be a black womyn!

This poem highlights the promise and potential of writing and sharing poetry with one another. Through sharing their thoughts, experiences, and ideologies, students were able to explore and step into their full humanity, see others recognize that humanity, and begin healing from some of the harms they have experienced. Through this process, students expressed love and empathy, and felt loved in return. It is these conditions that led these two girls to write an impromptu poem in which they were eager to affirm themselves and their peers.

Poetry and poetic performances are an important way to honor and incorporate the literary legacy of communities of color. While meeting all Common Core standards, this curricular unit offers an important method for students to find and utilize their voices. More so, it is an important humanizing literacy practice that lends itself to the healing necessary for communities constantly under attack. In relation, Sharim and Cam practiced critically caring literacy pedagogies, which is a concept that will be explored in the following chapter. Social justice teachers in urban schools have a responsibility to create the conditions for young people to practice speaking their truth within the context of the classroom setting.

KEY IDEAS IN THIS CHAPTER

- Both Sharim and Cam, co-teachers of an eleventh- and twelfth-grade English class, saw schools as disconnected from their lived experiences and as institutions that silenced their voice and dehumanized them. Both turned to teaching in hopes of being the kind of teacher that they never had.
- Their poetry unit, titled "Word and World," was an example of teachers practicing critically caring literacy pedagogies to create learning opportunities for young people to understand the relationship between words, their world, and their lived experiences.
- Students composed and performed original poetry that was reflective and humanizing. Poetry allowed students to share and process parts of themselves that they had never discussed with the classroom community.

Chapter Six

Reflections on Sharim and Cam

Youth Voice, Student Literacies

Critically relevant pedagogy must be grounded in the adage, "Students do not care how much you know until they know how much you care." Cultivating culturally responsive caring over the span of three academic years was the context upon which the teaching practice in the previous chapter was based. To express caring, Sharim and Cam practiced Akom's (2003) suggestion that teachers respect and make use of students' cultural capital to transform perceptions of deficits in urban youth into potential cultural strengths.

In turn, the culturally responsive caring (Howard, 2002; Valenzuela, 1999) for the youth of color described in the previous chapter more effectively interested them in relevant forms of academic learning. In other words, culturally responsive caring was best communicated by the ways Sharim and Cam applied it to their pedagogy.

As such, Sharim and Cam wanted to not only use the performance poetry unit to build upon their students' critical cultural thinking but also to facilitate a process whereby students would be able to give words and voice to the experiences that were weighing on their mind and spirit. As such, the unit would not only help young people to critically analyze words through poetry but also equip them with the skills to use their words and to name their experiences in ways that would be both humanizing and healing for both the individual and the collective.

This approach to teaching was critical and culturally relevant because it drew on students' lived experiences and cultural ways of knowing in a process that was socially transformative. Ladson-Billings (1994/2009) asserts, "Culturally relevant teaching is a pedagogy that empowers students intellectually, socially, emotionally, and politically by using cultural referents to impart knowledge, skills, and attitudes" (p. 20).

Culturally relevant pedagogy rests on three propositions: (a) academic success; (b) cultural competence; and (c) "students must develop a critical consciousness through which they challenge the status quo of the current social order" (Ladson-Billings, 1995, p. 160). Essentially, critically relevant approaches to teaching informed Sharim and Cam's choosing loss of land, struggle with identity, toxic masculinity, exploitation of women, and queer love as topics in their performance poetry unit.

Identifying these topics as some of the most pressing concerns in their students' lives allowed Sharim and Cam to facilitate students' abilities to transition between and across their multiple identities, while developing in them an awareness of the world and their position in it.

Academic achievement and student learning are about teachers challenging students' minds so that they can improve their ability to think—to apply, analyze, synthesize, and evaluate information—in order to excel in schools. Cultural competence is the ability to help students grow in the knowledge and understanding of their own culture while typically acquiring skills in mainstream culture, which students use to navigate their own worlds in order to become socially, politically, and economically viable. Critical consciousness helps students understand that what they are learning is useful not only to them, but also for a larger social purpose.

As a form of culturally relevant pedagogy, critical pedagogy facilitates spaces where students "recognize and attempt to transform those undemocratic and oppressive features of hegemonic control that often structure everyday classroom existence in ways not readily apparent" (McLaren, 1994/2003, p. 78). Critical pedagogy taps into student agency by facilitating their critical social consciousness and raising awareness of the sociopolitical context in which it is embedded. Consequently, critical pedagogy goes beyond equity discourses that have tamed explicit liberation agendas in social justice education theory.

Along those lines, Giroux (1992) calls for teaching practices that reflect "a politics that is attentive to the material and human suffering exhibited in forms of domestic colonialism expressed in racial violence, shameful unemployment among Black youth, and the growing numbers of minorities who daily join the ranks of the hungry and homeless" (p. 19). Together, critically relevant pedagogies draw from students' cultural frameworks, lived experiences, and diverse learning styles to specifically engage "in the task of reframing, refunctioning, and reposing" (McLaren, 2000, p. 185) essential questions to transform power and knowledge relations.

FOSTERING STUDENTS' SOCIOCRITICAL LITERACIES

Sharim and Cam also applied literacy teaching frameworks that maximized students' abilities to read, write, think, and communicate in their own interests. In this way, their instructional unit fulfilled Gutierrez's (2008) call for sociocritical literacy by reconceptualizing "teaching and learning of literacy for poor and immigrant youth" (p. 148) by positing practices that draw from, not sanction against, students' "community cultural wealth" (Yosso, 2005).

Sharim and Cam drew from their students' "robust" literacies to connect their curricula to the needs of young people struggling to navigate culturally alienating schooling institutions and the harsh conditions of everyday life. Applying sociocritical literacy in the context of critically relevant pedagogy required that students read and write counter-narratives (Solórzano & Yosso, 2002) as an empowering means "toward critical social thought" (Gutierrez, 2008, p. 149). Sociocritical literacy also functioned as a "historicizing literacy that privileges and is contingent upon students' sociohistorical lives" and pays close "attention to contradictions in and between texts lived and studied . . . locally experienced and historically influenced" (Gutierrez, 2008, p. 149).

In academic contexts where both black and brown student school performance was negatively impacted by mainstream narratives and ideologies that constructed them as intellectually inferior, Cam and Sharim historicize everyday institutional literacy practices while leveraging these into powerful learning tools to foster more complex ways of reading and writing that are linguistically and culturally situated in school. Sociocritical literacy practices build on cultural knowledge to develop sophisticated literacy capacities and meaning-making processes.

This pedagogy also honors Freire and Macedo's (1987) position that young people must learn to read and write the world and the word so as to transform hostile social conditions that undermine their humanity. The architect of this framing, Paulo Freire (1970/1988), argued that literacy programs must be informed by "a radical pedagogy so that the students' language will cease to provide its speakers the experience of subordination and, moreover, may be brandished as a weapon of resistance to the dominance of standard language" (p. 154).

To practice a radical pedagogy, Perry, Steele, and Hilliard's (2003) indigenous African American philosophy of education is also relevant to the predominantly black student context within which this pedagogy was applied. They posed a pressing question relevant to other dispossessed communities: "Why should one focus on learning in school if that learning doesn't . . . have the capacity to affect, inform, or alter . . . one's status as a member of an oppressed group?" (p. 11).

Perry and colleagues answer this question in their final analysis by asserting that students must "[r]ead and write . . . as an act of resistance, as a political act, for racial uplift, so [they] can lead [their] people well in the struggle for liberation!" (p. 19). The theoretical purpose of this type of humanizing literacy is clear—critically relevant education confronts oppression, affirms the humanity of the learner, and uses literacy as a tool to transform their realities and subvert subjugation.

READING THE WORD AND THE WORLD

To identify the context-responsive needs of learners, Freire and Macedo (1987) maintained that critical literacy begins by correlating the practice of reading the word and the world. They argued that young people first learn to decipher the universe around them before accessing and developing a language to describe it. Critical literacy, from Freire's (1970/1988) perspective, results in the "transformation of . . . dehumanizing structure[s] . . . a difficult apprenticeship in naming [an oppressive] world" (p. 402).

Renaming the world requires that students learn to become critically conscious of how they construct their realities through precise words they use to describe it. In order to effectively develop the literacy capacity of our students, Freire and Macedo (1987) insisted "that words used in organizing a literacy program come from . . . the 'word universe' of people who are learning, expressing their actual language, their anxieties, fears, demands, and dreams" (p. 35). Such approaches tap into urban identities and local "street" discourses in ways that engage students as critical readers, writers, and oral communicators.

Moreover, reading the word and the world enables students to make sense of the harsh realities shaping much of their lived experience. The resulting "thought-language" reflects "the act of knowing through praxis, by which [learners] transform reality" (Freire, 1970/1988, p. 398). Humanizing literacy happens as teachers guide students to interrogate their multiple identities, the social conditions that define their worldviews, and communicate transformative readings of the word and the world.

Through these practices, critically responsive pedagogies and humanizing literacies draw from students' cultural frameworks and lived experiences to engage them in learning that nurtures caring relationships, reflecting concern for their lives outside of the classroom while illuminating and disrupting existing power relations.

KEY IDEAS IN THIS CHAPTER

- Critically relevant pedagogy is rooted first and foremost in teacher-student relationships, which are the foundations of learning through open communication grounded in care and trust.
- Central to critically relevant pedagogy are humanizing literacies, which guide students' learning through the literacies they already have.
- Critically relevant pedagogy is an effective pedagogy for all teachers, especially those in urban schools.

Chapter Seven

Routines for Liberation with Ms. A

Classroom Community in Third Grade

Abby Taheri-Woodworth teaches third grade in the diverse, working class Excelsior neighborhood of San Francisco. She was raised by an Iranian American mother outside of Detroit, experiencing the racial and gendered marginalization that accompanied the circumstances of her childhood. These lived experiences led her to education, specifically to the urban education and social justice program at University of San Francisco where she honed her desire to enact powerful social-justice teaching. This chapter—part ethnographic observation and part teacher personal narrative—is a close look at everyday life in a classroom. It reflects the continued work of Ms. A's action research and her quest to make the classroom a place where all students are learning from and with one another. As you shall see, it took some years for her to find the right balance, the right pedagogy and practice, to enact those values.

MORNING ACTIVITY IN MS. A'S CLASSROOM

The first thing one notices entering Ms. A's third-grade class is the atmosphere of purposeful activity—no kids running around, no teacher yelling, just students doing work, some on one project, some on another. Some students are preparing their own breakfasts, putting bagels in the microwaves on their own, while others are working on math problems.

Her classroom buzzes with activity, much of it student initiated, as one table is working on a presentation and another is sharing book reports with one other and a third is playing math games on computers. The teacher choreographs the movements but does not spend a great deal of time telling, downloading information. Her expression of social justice teaching is not primarily in the content, though on the wall one sees quotations from Maya Angelou, Lorraine Hansberry, Nelson Mandela, and Mahatma Gandhi, and on the bookshelf are books of every culture next to a student-generated set of science notebooks.

In reality, the most striking thing about her classroom is the pedagogy, the way of organizing the student community and orchestrating the tone and focus of activities. In this class, each student's home language and cultural discourse is recognized and communities of students of color are invited in. While the class certainly has students with learning disabilities, students enduring social traumas, and students still learning English, Ms. A manages to keep every student involved and challenged.

Ms. A moves from table to table. She talks to Carmen over a hurdle in her math problem and chats with Charles about the discussion she had with his mother last night. Ms. A looks up and says, "Who still needs time to eat? Just do your tens, OK?" Kids are still moving freely around the classroom, from one task to another. Finally, after about twenty minutes, Ms. A plays a tone on the harmonica and the students come to the rug. "Take your circle spots," she reminds the students. She speaks to the students:

> Two things happened to me this morning: one, I had a very hard time getting out of bed, I was so sleepy! But two, I got an email from Lizard this morning, who we met on our field trip. All it said was "wow wow wow wow wow wow," and she said it was so great to meet this class. I was getting out of my car and Gardner Gray had a card for us. "Hey, friends, I wanted to say thank you. I was having such a hard time on Monday. But you all cheered me up so much I finished the day smiling." Let's have a clap for us.

Some students are squirming, some distracted, but nothing rises to what are considered "management" issues. Ms. A adds, "I was noticing that other people like being around our class." What appreciations do you have for the class?

Quickly students shout out their thoughts:

- I appreciate the class because they did a good job at the garden;
- for learning and behaving well;
- because we always have a good time making friends;
- because everybody here listens and is nice to each other;
- everybody has a positive attitude, not selfish, wants everyone to have fun;
- selfless;
- because everybody cheers me up;
- we make other people happy;
- if there's a problem we solve it;

- when you see someone playing by themselves, always include them;
- the way that Ms. A teaches us;
- nice and making new friends;
- everybody does not fight too much and they don't have a lot of attitude;
- because all do a good job;
- when kinders or first graders are being bad, we teach them to be good;
- whenever anybody is hurt, we help them out.

"OK," Ms. A announces, "LeShay, choose a game." LeShay chooses Sheep and Shepherds. And they all jump in.

BUILDING TRUST

This is the atmosphere in Ms. A's classroom all day. It is not always easy, though, and there are many struggles and challenges behind the curtain. Reflecting on her pedagogy, Ms. A argues that a strong positive classroom community is the most important part of her classroom. It is what she puts the most thought into before school starts. She recognizes that learning can't happen until everyone in the classroom community trusts each other.

During her action research project as a part of the UESJ program, Ms. A developed the idea of a "justice relevant curriculum . . . to teach the combined impact of individual and group movements for change in order to address the needs and lived experiences of the very diverse groups of students in schools as well as to work towards solidarity building." This research, she decided, would center both on the kinds of materials they studied but also on how the classroom community supported each other.

Ms. A shares this:

> The notion of authentic caring, as described by Valenzuela (1999) is about caring on the deeply personal level, including valuing the cultural identities of students and families. Valenzuela describes connection, unconditional love, and thorough understanding of the other as vital components to authentic care . . . Authentic care, like culturally relevant teaching, must "follow from and flow through relationships cultivated between teacher and student" and involves critical reflection on whether your interactions as an educator are adding to or subtracting from each student's positive experiences at school.
>
> In a commitment to community care, this relationship cannot exist without including the essential element of family. The student, if experiencing authentic care, is more likely to feel safe and secure to disclose their true self. It is not only the responsibility of educators to demonstrate caring towards their students, but to also create a culture of caring where students develop the capacity to care for one another, people in their communities, and people in the world.

Further, as she thinks about her time in the classroom now, she reflects:

Each year at back to school night, I tell myself not to cry. And every year, I cry. Back to school night comes a couple weeks into the school year when I honestly don't know or love my kids the way I know that I will by the end of the year. My journal generally reads that I'm exhausted, and I wonder why they're way behind academically, and so so chatty. That's not why I'm crying, though. I inevitably tear up as I tell my students' parents how much I love what I do; how brilliant I think these students are; how much I care for them and want them to learn everything that is going to give them whatever opportunities they want. I think that that underlying principle and overwhelming feeling is a lot of what creates such a wonderful community in my class. I trust my students to be great people and they live up to that. For some of my students, it takes time. I have had kids tell me that they'd never liked themselves until third grade. I had a student a couple years ago, Gabriel, who told the class at the end of third grade that he had never known how to be kind and that that was the best thing he learned in third grade.

LOOKING BACK ON BEING A FIRST-YEAR TEACHER

It did not always go so smoothly. Ms. A's first year of teaching was incredibly challenging and almost broke her and pushed her out of the profession. But she was learning what it means to be a social justice educator in a high-poverty, high-trauma school with a diverse community and as a teacher who comes from a different world in many ways.

Recognizing that teaching historically disenfranchised students is a political act, she sought to dismantle every aspect of her classroom that could ever be compared to a prison, reacting to the very real school-to-prison pipeline. For example, students were allowed to make their own decisions about where they sat, and the way they lined up and came to the rug was unstructured.

While some teachers refuse to give students pencils because they'd lost or broken them, Ms. A responded by going through hundreds of pencils in the first month of school. Whenever they needed one, they had one. In the beginning, wanting students to have a voice, everyone was talking all the time and mostly talking smack about each other. While she loved that first class, she now feels that in many ways she failed them with her oversimplified ideas of what they needed. Late in that first year, she was miserable. Students were getting in fights even in class, and she was putting out every fire and negotiating every problem for them. She remarks, "I provided them the opportunity to fail my expectations, because they weren't clear. And then I'd be mad."

"In the beginning," she remarks, "I wanted everybody to choose what they do. It was painful for me to have line order or it felt wrong to have rug spots. But they were physically fighting every time they came to the rug. And we'd have this big community breakdown where somebody felt unsafe. And it was my fault. I had learned what not to do as far as perpetuating oppression but I left it open and actually did not create structure that allows for independence."

She knows her students felt loved that year, and she felt love for them, but she feels that, in her inexperience, she did not create a very safe space or a space where a high level of academics could take place. Her initial approach also did not help them become better, more independent, or confident people. Students didn't need to take responsibility for their belongings or their actions because she would solve or help solve their problems as they came up.

Midway through the year, Ms. A did a reset. She created structures that would be good for the community, but that were also based around problems she had seen arise in her first attempts. "I realized I was mad that I was going through a box of pencils a day," so she created a system for keeping track of each student's pencil and with students being rewarded for that. Students practiced walking to the rug in ten seconds or less, forty or fifty times until they got it right. They walked to line quietly and quickly and she praised and praised and praised. She realized that when she wasn't stressed by the idea of a transition or a conversation, she could be much more positive and actually notice all the wonderful things happening in her class.

She reflects on that first, underdeveloped year: "I don't blame a social justice mind-set for this, but I think I was misguided in mine. I was so willing to address the realities of poverty and racism and a system that was built to fail these students that I forgot what everyone needs for success. In my anger at those systemic inequalities, I recreated a space where students couldn't be their best selves."

A structure for independence. That was Ms. A's epiphany, and she spent the second year developing such structures.

BUILDING CLASSROOM STRUCTURES FOR STUDENT AGENCY

Ms. A's new approach is a pedagogy centered on building students' agency. As will be discussed in chapter 8, her approach is in contrast to the routines of traditional schooling, which position the teacher as the authority and the students as passive recipients of knowledge. Ms. A's focus on agency is a core value for her. She trusts her students to be kind and look out for one other, to be their best selves. She works with them when that's not happening. She trusts her students to work hard and feel that working hard can be fun and exciting. These things allow students to make decisions that positively impact themselves and their classmates. She holds her students to high expectations—both academically and socially. With clear structures, her students, even the ones who have the hardest time in the beginning, meet this expectation.

Another example of her clear structures, which might seem counterintuitive, has to do with backpacks. She noticed that students wanted to go to their backpacks all the time during class, claiming they needed something or needed to check on something. But even in lower grades, there had been some issues with students stealing from one other.

It shocked people at times to come into her classroom and find large locks on the closet doors, with their backpacks inside. She didn't want students to feel like she was controlling their every action or that she didn't trust them, but the moment she started putting those locks on the closet doors was the moment she saw her students relax. They didn't need to worry about their belongings being taken. By the end of October, she didn't need to worry about locking the closets anymore and left them open. They had built the trust needed in class without being distracted by worry, and they knew that their things were safe.

She remarks,

> I think the number of structures in my classroom sometimes scares adults—even other teachers. In the beginning of the year there is an expectation and a structure for pencils, for phones, for notebooks, for lining up and for just about everything else in between. What I find, though, is that when students know what to expect, they start to self-regulate. The classroom isn't a scary place. Instead it's a place where they know exactly how to interact and react to a problem. And when that reaction doesn't meet the expectation, they already know what the consequence will be. And I already know what the consequence will be, which means that in a high stress environment, I can maintain my calm most of the time. It takes so much pressure off of me and I think, in return, takes a lot of pressure off of the students.
>
> This might sound basic, but I also find it incredibly important to get to know my students and find that this builds their trust with me. It's one thing for me to trust them, but it's probably more important for them to trust me. In the first week of school, I text or call each family two or three times to tell them what a great week it's been (even when it's been a serious struggle) and how excited I am to be their child's teacher along with one or two anecdotes. I spend the first week of recesses outside with my students, watching how they interact and playing with them, even though I have a million little things to do in my room.

STUDENT PORTFOLIO WRITING AS A FORM OF COMMUNITY BUILDING

Back in her classroom, Ms. A reminds the students, "In our writing portfolios, we have finished chapter 1, finished with chapter 2, and we are editing chapter 3. Now we are on to chapter 4, which is our compare and contrast chapter. Tomorrow, what comes after planning?"

"Drafting!"

She reminds students, "Every chapter needs a topic sentence. Turn and talk about what you want to accomplish with a topic sentence."

After some spirited discussion, she sounds a tune on the harmonica and asks students to share. They offer explanations for what they want their topic sentence to be:

- "It gets a reader's mind ready for reading about whatever the chapter is about."
- "It usually looks like ask a question and then answer it."
- "It captures the curiosity of the reader."

Students rehearse some sentence starters for topic sentences:

- Do you like ___? Then you'll like ___.
- Have you ever wondered what the difference between ___ and ___ is?
- There are many similarities between ___ and ___.

They then Venn diagram for their compare and contrast essay, identifying the differences and similarities between two things that they intend to compare.

As students strategize two things they want to compare, they are clearly practicing explicit and self-aware thinking at a sophisticated level. On this day, it includes observing their subjects closely and describing what exists in the two groups being compared; building explanations and interpretations of the actions; making connections; wondering and asking questions; and going below the surface of things.

The topic plans come tumbling out:

- How some babies are similar and how each is unique and different
- The difference between babies and dogs
- Soccer compared to American football
- Dogs versus cats
- Minecraft versus Roblox

Students meet one-on-one with Ms. A, discussing their ideas and planning next steps in their writing. "Write down your ideas in bullet points," she reminds them. "Right now you are just planning."

One group of students decide that both dogs and babies do the following:

- Poop when they shouldn't
- Have to be fed

- Need to be cleaned

Ms. A says, as an aside, "If you were doing dogs versus cats, clean would be a difference." Students laugh.

Then students work to match their differences.

"Hmm, well," Artemis remarks to her partner, "I'm thinking that dogs play fetch and babies play with baby toys; dogs wear a leash and collar, babies wear diapers." Students think through their categories, all the while sharing with partners.

SPECIFIC CLASSROOM ACTIVITIES FOR BUILDING COMMUNITY

Ms. A and her teaching partner have been intentional about creating community from the beginning of the year. They developed a series of values with the students, and these values are evident in the work every day. Her values, really a map of social justice community building, are summed up.

A) Our Brains Grow When We Make Mistakes. We Ask Questions When We Don't Understand.

During the activity students think of a time when something was really hard for them. Each student thinks of a word that describes how they felt then and writes it down on a piece of paper. Then Ms. A talks about how when something is hard for them, their brains work extra hard to figure it out, and those are the times that their brain is growing. They talk about synapses and that when something is easy, their synapses don't have to fire as much, and their brains don't grow.

They then crinkle up the paper with their word about being frustrated and jump up and down on it. Then they open up the paper and look at all the little lines and she describes that those are like the synapses. Students then trace the lines and think about when they feel frustrated, their brains are growing the most if they work through it.

B) We Appreciate that We All Learn in Different Ways.

They take a multiple intelligences survey and share the different ways they like to learn.

C) We Grow the Most When We Work Together.

Students work in table groups on a fun activity. They have a lot of cups and need to stack them in a triangle. Students can't use their hands, though, and are given one rubber band with five strings coming from it. They have to figure out how to stack the cups using only the strings and one rubber band.

D) We Recognize that Our Actions Affect Our Community.

Ms. A has demonstrated this value in a number of different ways. Sometimes students act out skits about incidents that have happened at school before. Or they play a game where everyone holds a piece of a string and tries to untangle it. When one person pulls on the string, other kids feel that pull.

E) We Work Hard to Nurture Our Relationships and We Repair Them When Needed.

During this time, they go over the restorative practices and questions. They talk about how to solve conflicts and what it feels like to have conflict.

LITERACY AND STUDENTS' STRENGTHS

While it sounds so simple, so fundamental, creating community, recognizing and honoring the humanity of each student, is central to social justice pedagogy and radically subversive to the authoritarian models that have been dominant in US education. It means attending to the group and also noticing and caring for each student's individual concerns. Ms. A calls the students into a circle.

"We're going to squeeze in one chapter. Remember she showed her the spell book? They went back to Bean's house to get the worms to put the spell on Nancy."

She begins to read from the book. Then, in a quick aside, "Carrie, sweetheart, can you check your blood sugar? Wash your hands first."

Then to the class, "Why do you think Nancy's crying? Turn and talk." And on it goes.

She reflects on her expectations of students:

> I think my students are brilliant, and I find that if I hold them to that brilliance, they meet me there. Overall, academically, there is a really big range in my class each year. That being said, their thinking, I believe, is advanced. This is particularly true when we're reading and writing about things that they feel are relevant to their lives. We ended the school year writing opinion essays and students had so much to say—about Trump, LGBTQ rights, gun violence, littering, and a variety of other topics.
>
> I love teaching math, and I find that my students love learning math. Although many come in far behind in math and struggle with some foundational skills, I feel that the majority are able to work through a difficult unknown problem. Every student in my class shows perseverance in solving

problems, which, in my mind, is a really important component in understanding math.

BUILDING COMMUNITY AND SOCIAL JUSTICE PEDAGOGY

Ms. A considers building community an art:

> I realized something important about social justice education and liberatory education. These students experience more daily trauma, both microaggressions and macroaggressions, than anything I could imagine. Each year, I've had students who have a parent in jail, a parent who has been deported or fears being deported, students who have witnessed murders (sometimes of a family member).
>
> My students live in San Francisco, Vallejo, Fairfield, Oakland. They are doubled and tripled up in one- or two-bedroom apartments. Their families work hard, love their kids, and want the best for them. I've realized that many of my students worry. A lot. They worry about deportations and shootings and having enough to eat. And I realized that as a social justice educator, it is my most important job to make sure that they don't worry about school. I have found that, for me, creating a safe and fun space means having more structures instead of fewer.

In her classroom, justice relevant curriculum and teaching means attending to the students who are in front of her, to their particular needs, their ways of knowing, and their unique journeys in life. Socially transformative pedagogy is built upon this foundation because it is centered on students' lives, as the classroom constructs its own culture of engagement and thriving.

KEY IDEAS IN THIS CHAPTER

- As a UESJ student, Abby Taheri-Woodworth began developing justice relevant curriculum as part of her action research project. This curriculum sought to teach the impact of individual and group movements for social change as a way of addressing the various needs of her students while building classroom community and solidarity.
- Ms. A reflects on her first few years of teaching, and ultimately concludes that having more classroom structures allow for greater student agency and community.
- Through building community and focusing on student agency, Ms. A's classroom becomes a space in which student learning is organic, creative, cooperative, and student-centered.

Chapter Eight

Reflections on Ms. A

Revisiting the Purpose of Schooling

Ms. A's teaching is based on her continued refinement of the justice relevant curriculum that she initiated through her action research project as a new teacher. Her classroom is a space that fosters authentic, meaningful learning for so many different students, and her reflection on the evolution of this journey shows that socially transformative pedagogy is a process. It involves building trust, honoring student agency, and—perhaps most important—failing. Ms. A's classroom and her reflections on her early years of teaching showcase the ways that the question "Why?" must continually impact our teaching—why are we learning this, why am I teaching this way, and why is education the way it is?

In reflecting on these questions, it is important to understand where the "common sense" of schooling practice comes from. What are the factors that led to today's educational system? And why is Ms. A's third grade classroom so drastically different from others in her building and across the nation?

Certainly, free public education has been claimed as a core value of American society, but what led American society to this current era of standardization, testing, and inequitable educational opportunity in US public schools? And what are some of the historical factors that generated the structural rifts in American educational culture?

FOUNDATIONS OF AMERICAN PUBLIC EDUCATION

In all human societies, children are inducted into the cultural practices, the sign systems, the productive skills, and the values through formal and informal educational projects. How is it that the United States has come to a position where such induction, such preparation, is so flawed that most young people are not allowed to enter into a successful economic and social participation in society? How have American schools, which proclaim themselves to be a color-blind meritocracy, become institutions that churn out failure and ejection for black and brown students, for low-income students, for immigrant students, and for gender non-conforming students?

In order to answer these questions, it is necessary to look back on the founding of public schools and their purpose. In the colonial occupation population of North America, education was always reserved for the elite—and no Indians, no Africans, no immigrants, and no farmers were expected to attend school at all.

But with the rising immigrant population in the nineteenth century, reformers like Horace Mann called for "common schools" to assimilate immigrant workers into American Protestant values—essentially, to make them good workers. While the elite were expected to be exposed to deep reflection and complex skills designed to help them rule, the emphasis for the lower classes was on discipline, compliance, and narrow tasks. Indeed, authoritarian, top-down education has always been the default mode of public education.

At the same time, however, we have seen another kind of education, a parallel track of learning that has been subversive and often underground. Schoolhouses in the slave quarters, for example, were initiated by captives who understood that their liberation was related to their ability to achieve literacy. And cultures of resistance, from gospel music to collective dance to outright escape, were also taught in community-based centers (Perry et al., 2003).

Particularly telling in the official schools has been the civilizing mission of education, which found its ugliest side in the Carlisle Indian School, founded by Colonel Richard Pratt in Pennsylvania during the same time as the Indian extermination wars in the American west. The goal of the school was to isolate students from tribal life, to keep them under constant surveillance in order to police "savage" behavior, and to build values of individuality versus community identification. Pratt testified in 1892:

> A great general has said that the only good Indian is a dead one, and that high sanction of this destruction has been an enormous factor in promoting Indian massacres. In a sense, I agree with the sentiment, but only in this: that all the

Indian there is in the race should be dead. Kill the Indian in him, save the man. (p. 260)

Histories like these point to the colonial use of education, furthering not liberation but domination.

General Samuel Armstrong played a similar role as the founder of Hampton Institute in 1868 for the "uplifting and civilizing" of black workers in Virginia (Watkins, 2001). A few years after Hampton opened, he wrote this:

> This is no easy machine to run wisely, rightly. The darkies are so full of human nature and have to be most carefully watched over. They are apt to be possessed with strange notions. To simply control them is one thing, but to educate, to draw them out, to develop the germ of good possibilities into firm fruition, requires the utmost care. (Watkins, 2001, p. 49)

With both Pratt and Armstrong, we see the imposition of a panopticon of total surveillance in order to guard against native cultural practices (Foucault, 1977).

Throughout the nineteenth century, well-meaning, middle-class white women often took it upon themselves to travel long distances in order to "bring education" to the oppressed—whether this was in the Freedman schools in the south after the Civil War or in the new schools the United States set up in the Philippines after seizing that country from Spain. While they sought to spread education as a virtuous aid, their work primarily played the role of handmaiden to violent domination.

But Sitting Bull (Teton Sioux), whose people were subject to the Carlisle School, had this rejoinder to white schooling efforts: "If the Great Spirit had desired me to be a White man, he would have made me so in the first place. He put in your heart certain wishes and plans; in my heart he put other and different desires. Each man is good in the sight of the Great Spirit. It is not necessary, that eagles should be crows" (1883, p. 2).

Throughout the nineteenth century, US public schools continued to expand, with legal segregation in place. Education leaders adopted the business model of organization perfected in the industrial revolution. Schools were designed by scientific management and social efficiency experts. The ideological underpinnings of pedagogy were established by Social Darwinists, influenced by the new sociology of Herbert Spencer, who saw education as preparing the privileged for domination and the poor for service.

While progressives like John Dewey and black activists like W. E. B. Du Bois argued for a child-centered pedagogy based on experience and social construction of knowledge, the dominant form of school organization was informed by business rationalism and authoritarianism. By the early twentieth century, the factory-model school dominated educational planning.

ESTABLISHING CRITICAL PEDAGOGY IN US SCHOOLS

Throughout the twentieth century, the question of how to organize schooling has been key to the struggle for democracy. Chinese, Mexican American, and African American communities fought protracted legal and organizing battles against school segregation and exclusion. In addition, in cases such as the Freedom Schools in Mississippi in the 1960s, critical pedagogy was developed as part of the struggle for freedom. This pedagogy was founded in direct confrontation to and contestation of the assimilationist ideals discussed above. It named the structural hierarchies and racism at the core of the educational system that students were experiencing.

Charles Cobb, alongside Ella Baker of the Student Nonviolent Coordinating Committee (SNCC), wrote a brief proposal for Freedom Schools in the community organizing work in Mississippi. They explained that while the black children in the South were denied many things—decent school facilities, honest and forward-looking curriculum, fully qualified teachers—the fundamental injury was "a complete absence of academic freedom, and students are forced to live in an environment that is geared to squashing intellectual curiosity, and different thinking" (Cobb, 1963, p. 67).

Cobb named the classrooms of Mississippi as "intellectual wastelands," and he challenged himself and others "to fill an intellectual and creative vacuum in the lives of young Negro Mississippi, and to get them to articulate their own desires, demands and questions" (67). Their own desires, their own demands, their own questions—for African Americans living in semifeudal bondage, managed and contained through a system of law and custom as well as outright terror, such freedom required a leap of imagination and daring.

The aim of the Freedom School curriculum was to challenge the students' curiosity about the world, support appreciation of their particularly "Negro" cultural background, and teach basic literacy skills in one integrated program. That is, the students would study problems arising in their own world, such as the administration of justice or the relationship between state and federal authority. Each problem area would be built around a specific episode which was close to the experience of the students—an early example of socially transformative pedagogy in action.

The approach of the Freedom Schools corresponds exactly with the education model Paulo Freire (1970) was developing in Brazil. In the US rural South and in the global south, organizers recognized that wisdom and leadership resided in the experience of the poorest and most marginalized in society. Instead of posing a top-down, information transmission model, these educators insisted that curriculum must be co-constructed by the students and rooted in their own interests. Students' experiences and their insights were a driving force in the matters that students and teachers inquired into and the projects they undertook.

Liberatory education located the curriculum within the work—and play—of the classroom. Freire and Cobb both approached education as a matter of community organizing, community empowerment, and not simply the transmission of static knowledge from above. The thread of this approach has been included in the work of SNCC veteran Bob Moses in the Algebra Project. Others who elaborated these and similarly liberationist views included A. S. Neill, Lisa Delpit, Sylvia Ashton-Warner, Carol Lee, Herb Kohl, Maxine Greene, and many more. We can see that this stream of thinking, this educational practice, is the tradition that informs Ms. A's class.

REPRODUCTION AND RESISTANCE IN TODAY'S SCHOOLS

The contestation over the purpose of education continues today and is often played out daily—particularly in urban public schools—where divergent viewpoints from parents, school board members, administrators, teachers, and students clash. And while the liberatory models described above do exist, schools remain largely oppressive for working class youth of color in this country.

As argued throughout this book, schools are quite successful at reproducing the inequities of society, at pretending to offer a meritocracy while in fact presenting a stacked deck to marginalized communities, whose students seem to always be pushed out or failed. Thus, the often referred to "achievement gap" is simply a novel term for a problem that is decades old. More problematic than the data that such a gap refers to, however, is the lack of a critical analysis that unveils the root causes of such discrepancies in students' school experiences. Quite simply, the US education system is failing many students and it has done so since its inception.

In today's context, we see that schools are sites of aggressive intervention by forces of privatization and by entrepreneurs who see education as one of the next big markets, a chance to take tax money for private gains. Many of these schools—especially those that claim to serve low-income students—double down on the assumption that poor kids and students of color simply need more discipline and more control in order to bring test scores up. Far from empowering students, these school projects assume that white-middle-class discourse and core knowledge is the unassailable gold standard, that the task of schools is to dominate and control these outsiders; to "civilize the savages."

This authoritarian trend in education is found in well-funded foundations such as Broad and Walton, in nonprofits like Teach for America, and in many of the corporate charter schools. Federal government initiatives from the misnamed No Child Left Behind to the appropriately neoliberal Race to the Top to the generalizing Common Core have all advanced the narrative that the problem in schools and the lack of opportunities for students are caused by ineffective teachers, to imperfect information transmission projects.

The deleterious effects of deficit thinking, which Yosso (2005) calls "one of the most prevalent forms of contemporary racism in U.S. schools" (p. 75), continues to haunt the classroom today. As a response to this deficit thinking, Ms. A is determined to build asset-based approaches to curriculum and pedagogy that display students' cultural, linguistic, and educational strengths.

Ms. A practices an asset-based pedagogy not through a teacher-centered unit of study per se, but rather through building a classroom space that fosters students learning from and with one another. Her classroom is not bound by a seating chart and she does not base her assessment of students on state-mandated test scores. The classroom is a place for learning—for her and for her students.

It is through this type of subversive practice and socially transformative pedagogy that hope arises. While schools have crushed hope for years, they are also sites of contention and struggle. They are spaces for working out and debating what kind of future society is to be constructed and what exactly is the meaning of democracy. This is the arena these teachers have chosen to work in, to organize with community needs and aspirations at the center.

We see in classrooms in San Francisco's Excelsior District, the city's Mission District, in East Oakland, and in schools and communities on the ground all over the United States that powerful and meaningful educational work continues to advance. While these teacher-activists don't have the big megaphone, they are making a difference every day. In actions such as test refusal, in the Chicago and Oakland teachers' strikes of 2014 and 2019, in empowering projects and networks, poor people are demanding real community control of schools through the equitable distribution of resources as well as a curriculum and pedagogy that is responsive and meaningful to communities.

This community-based activism is the space of empowerment against the dominant narrative and is where classrooms powered by socially transformative pedagogy thrive. In such classrooms, community assets, and liberation come first. This pedagogy not only forwards the agency of students, but also, it curiously helps them navigate the gatekeepers of the system. Even as they critique these gatekeepers, challenge the set-up game, many of these students choose to move ahead in school and in higher education, succeeding in opposition to, not in compliance with, the authoritarian school forces.

The students we are encountering in these schools attest to this power struggle in the classroom and in communities. This tension is the ground zero in the struggles for education today.

KEY IDEAS IN THIS CHAPTER

- Throughout history, education has been used to indoctrinate native people into white supremacy and to assimilate immigrant workers into US industrialism.
- Concurrently, there are examples of historically oppressed groups resisting the factory model of schooling through a critical pedagogy that is connected to students' cultural backgrounds, their curiosity about the world, and the importance of literacy.
- Where there is oppression, there is resistance: teacher- and community-based activism continues to resist deficit thinking by prioritizing community assets and liberation.

Chapter Nine

Socially Transformative Pedagogy and the Tasks for Urban Teachers

The neoliberal agenda in education—the threats to education evident in the mania for standardized testing, the drive for privatization through charters and vouchers, and the turn toward emergency managers—makes teaching and learning a politically embattled project.

While many systems of oppression—extensive poverty, lack of jobs, inadequate housing, crippling health care costs, afflictions of violence and drugs—call out for attention, the neoliberal narrative insists that a "good" education would solve everything. Students would go to college, great jobs would be generated, the economy would thrive—problem solved.

But in reality this narrative is more sinister: it ignores the scourging intersections of racism, sexism, gender non-binary phobia, classism, and ableism—it ignores structural violence (Farmer et al., 2006), and it does not challenge current societal relations. And, in addition to ignoring these barriers to equity, it happily reproduces them while claiming the US education system to be a meritocracy.

THE PRESSURES FACING TEACHERS TODAY

The current US secretary of education, Betsy DeVos, is a billionaire "education reformer" and one of the country's most fierce advocates for the privatization of public schools. She ardently pushes for school vouchers and charter schools—including for-profit charters, deregulation of charters, and "right to work" laws that have weakened teachers' unions.

Through this type of leadership, the neoliberal agenda is furthered. And through the narrative it proliferates, many teachers—and especially new teachers—are trapped in a rigidly scrutinized pedagogical reality where the value of the work they do every day is questioned. Their success is largely determined by standardized tests, and they often enter schools in which preparing students to succeed on standardized tests is expected to be the sole focus of their teaching (Borrero, Flores, & De La Cruz, 2016; Kincheloe, 2008). These tests and this kind of training do not prepare students to be creative and powerful in solving problems but rather they are taught and expected to become passive cogs in a larger economy controlled by others (Meier & Knoester, 2017).

When students, and particularly students of color, do not add "value" to their standardized test-score profiles, there are both explicit and implicit consequences. In the classroom, the result is often more tests—or certainly more preparation for tests (Spring, 2004). Additionally, there is an inherent blaming that occurs—a blame focused on students and their families as well as teachers (Kumashiro, 2012). The system marginalizes students designated as losers in the game and channels them into life outside of the official economy, into detention and control, the school-to-prison pipeline.

Combined, these results leave our already underfunded urban public schools stripped of many of the elements that encourage students' critical thinking and creativity such as art, science, social studies, music, physical education, and technology. In addition, this emphasis on testing prioritizes predetermined outcomes. Many new teachers find themselves obliged to enact a pedagogy of poverty (Haberman, 2010) based on standards-aligned, context irrelevant textbooks, worksheets, and activities from scripted curricula.

The problem here is that teachers are being deprofessionalized. All the skills and pedagogical knowledge that make teaching effective, that inspires and transforms the lives of children, are more and more forbidden. By emphasizing predetermined outcomes, policies drive creativity and inquiry out of the classroom. A pedagogy of poverty undermines relational, dialogic, and investigative learning. In place of student-centered, culturally relevant, democratic, and socially transformative education, which has proven to be the most engaging approach to encourage critical thinking and initiative, teachers are reduced to academic clerks. This is an approach that neither drew them to the profession nor brings them a sense of worth as professionals.

TEACHER ATTRITION

As a result of this constrained professional identity, as well as low pay, fewer and fewer college graduates in the United States are choosing teaching as a career. College graduates saw the impact of the 2008 recession on teaching: stagnant pay, declining working conditions, larger class sizes, and job insecurity amid massive layoffs. It is no wonder that applications for teacher education programs are down over 50 percent over the past decade (Westervelt, 2015).

While it is important to focus on ways to improve teacher recruitment in times of a teacher shortage, reducing teacher attrition would have the greatest impact (Darling-Hammond et al., 2016). Teacher attrition rates are higher in the United States than in other countries where not only are teacher wages more competitive and working conditions more supportive, but also the general esteem and respect for educators is greater. More specifically, the teacher attrition rate nationwide hovers around 8 percent, and an additional 8 percent leave their current school. This rate is over double that of nations like Finland and Singapore, where 3 percent to 4 percent of teachers leave their job yearly (Carver-Thomas & Darling-Hammond, 2017).

At so-called hard-to-staff schools, turnover is dramatically higher. Today, barely 50 percent of new teachers in urban school districts last beyond five years in the profession. In these schools and districts, many teachers are often encouraged to enter teaching without having completed training and are hired through alternative certification programs like Teach For America, or with interim or emergency credentials. These alternatively certified teachers are 20 percent more likely to leave their schools, and two and a half times more likely to leave schools with a majority of students of color (Darling-Hammond et al., 2016).

Despite evidence that teacher attrition rates are higher among teachers with alternative credentials, school districts continue to form partnerships with programs like Teach for America and The New Teacher Project to recruit teachers. These programs tend to break down neighboring graduate programs that offer more training and support through building stronger relationships, greater commitments, and deeper frameworks rooted in critical theory and social justice.

Regardless of whether a teacher came through an alternative certification method or not, students in our country's urban schools are bearing the brunt: "the turnover rate in Title I schools is nearly 50 percent greater than that of non-Title I schools" (Darling Hammond et al., 2016, p. 44). In schools with mostly students of color, nearly 20 percent of English language learner, special education, and math and science teachers leave the profession or the school annually.

What is at the root of these high attrition rates? Urban teachers work under conditions which are largely unsustainable—classrooms of thirty-plus students; no living wage; lack of structured and rigorous support for English language learners, special education students, and students experiencing trauma; low degree of individual instructional autonomy; and limited decision-making influence. Teachers report problems with these conditions and administrative support, as well as a low pay.

Overall, 55 percent of teachers report leaving the profession because of dissatisfaction, with an additional 31 percent leaving to pursue another profession, and another 18 percent for financial reasons. Within the category of dissatisfaction, the number one complaint by teachers was being hemmed in by standardized testing and a dumbed-down, test-prep curriculum.

Today US teachers have more teaching hours, more students, and less planning time than most other teachers in the world. Thirty-six states are spending less than what they spent in 2007 on public education and that number will continue to go down under the current administration. Teacher salaries have lost ground, and in more than thirty states, teachers actually qualify for federal aid despite often having attained a master's degree.

These factors—when added to the historical and institutional legacies of struggle in US public schools—make teaching in today's urban classrooms a daunting undertaking. In essence, teaching as a profession is under attack and the solution proposed by those in power is the deprofessionalization of teaching and the marketization of public schools. And those left to bear this burden are teachers—experiencing the pressures from administrators, parents, and a national discourse that questions their efficacy, all while pursuing the life-altering work of engaging youth for eight hours each day.

TEACHER SUSTAINABILITY

What research, policy reports, and the national narrative fail to capture are the ways that teachers' livelihoods—their health, financial security, and emotional well-being—are also under attack. Teachers of color are forced to come to terms with teaching in an institution that has historically oppressed those who look just like them and their students. Through the outright exclusion or elimination of their native culture and the valuing of white supremacy, schools are places that attack any critical teacher's core. The schools that urban teachers enter every day put them on the defensive.

Teaching in schools that have intentionally been designed to make failure and competition almost inevitable for young people forces teachers to grapple with their purpose in exhausting ways. Teachers who see teaching and social justice as a part of their identity and not just their job find it infuriating to work in schools under school leaders who state that they care for all students (and even tout equity as a value) but then direct their schools in ways that center students who are already—by design—doing well, and push out—both willfully or through disregard—those who are not.

Because of such leadership—and the confines of an educational system that prioritizes white, middle-class values—teachers are left to deal with the reality that they are part of an institution that by design upholds hegemony. Their students and their families are being pushed out of rapidly gentrifying cities onto the streets or into multiple-family apartments while dealing with addiction, sexual harassment, gun violence, fear of deportation, loss of health care, or the transition into an uninviting political climate as immigrant refugees under the Trump administration.

Given these realities, urban teachers often carry with them the trauma of their students (Ginwright, 2016). This vicarious trauma follows teachers home and occupies them beyond school walls. They report losing sleep over it, having nightmares about it, and going home to cry about it. To provide a specific example, a local teacher that recently experienced a school shooting right as school was letting out had to scramble to get students into her classroom before closing and locking her door. She recalls the sudden almost freeze that her body took as she assessed the situation and realized it was likely that she was about to lose her life for and with these students. Months later, she still carries with her the fear she saw in her students' faces and the fear she experienced that day.

Another teacher was the first at the scene when her student got stabbed at a park across the street from their high school. In a fury, she used her scarf to hold the blood as her student's arm dangled and bled while people surrounded her. She feared that the student might lose her hand. In reflecting on this experience, she stresses how she wishes she could support her students in all the ways she know they need—even those which are beyond her control—because she sees the toll it takes on them.

Teachers are overwhelmed by the many roles they must take on to serve their students. They carry that weight and sooner or later the stresses are too great to handle. This is teaching when working with students who are the most targeted by oppression. This is why teacher education must strive to embed systems that help teachers also heal and maintain hope. And for all of these reasons, urban teachers need to have self-care embedded into their preparation and into the profession.

In states across the country, teacher induction programs—professional development and mentoring initiatives designed to support new teachers during their initial years of full-time teaching—have gained more attention and funding in an effort to increase teacher retention and support. Yet from the authors' experiences with these programs in local districts and from the feedback new teachers have shared, most induction programs as they are currently designed do not provide the kinds of meaningful support teachers want and need.

For example, new teachers often talk about their participation in such programs as an obligation—an added workload that feels more evaluative than supportive. Instead of providing structures for mentorship and collegiality—which most new teachers desperately want—induction programs often become another hoop for new teachers to jump through on their way to earning their teaching credential.

In socially just teacher communities across the country, like-minded professionals, practitioners, and community organizations are collaborating to provide spaces for teachers to process the above, unaddressed social stress that their districts, schools, nor teacher training programs have taken up. Community groups like People's Education Movement, with chapters in the San Francisco Bay Area, Los Angeles, and Chicago; New York Collective of Radical Educators; the Education for Liberation national network; Educators' Network for Social Justice in Milwaukee; Teacher Activist Groups (TAG) in Philadelphia and Boston; Northwest Teaching for Social Justice (NWTSJ) in Portland and Seattle; Teachers for Social Justice (TSJ) in Chicago; and San Francisco's Teachers 4 Social Justice (T4SJ) provide models for districts, schools, and teacher training programs from which to learn.

These grassroots spaces seek to identify and address the most pressing concerns of teachers, students, and communities in their local contexts and aim to create sustainable educational spaces to promote pedagogical growth, radical healing, and social transformation—more of which the profession needs to offer teachers in urban schools, teachers of color, critically conscious teachers, and teachers who experience the intersections of oppression amidst the status quo structures of schooling.

They have each slowly built, through conversations after collective conversations, progressive, multiracial spaces to bring teachers into critically supportive environments; created counterspaces for professional development so that teacher dialogue is prioritized; and organized discussions on context responsive pedagogy among collectives of socially transformative teachers. The UESJ program strives to do this. Collectively, UESJ, in line with these groups, works to bring about changes to the systems, expectations, and practices that are described throughout this book.

TEACHERS AS LEADING CHANGE AGENTS

As discussed in the introductory chapter to this book, while the suggestion that education would fix everything is enough of a distortion, this same public narrative finds an easy scapegoat in teachers, who apparently are failing to advance the economic recovery magic by being ineffective, incompetent, and even lazy (e.g., Ayers et al., 2018; Kumashiro, 2012). As Donald Trump (2000) has argued,

> It's a straightforward clash of issues: The Brotherhood of Blackboard Workers wants to keep the door closed to competition. That way they can run things as they choose, without review. And we've got to bring on the competition— open the schoolhouse doors and let parents choose the best school for their children. Education reformers call this school choice, charter schools, vouch-

ers, even opportunity scholarships. I call it competition—the American way. (p. 1)

In order to act on the side of youth and communities, teachers inevitably subvert the dominant paradigm of education. The UESJ project at the University of San Francisco focuses on building a practice of socially transformative pedagogy with its teachers. Through action research projects, new teachers develop habits and skills of critical reflection, a cycle of inquiry, and accountability to the broader community.

Socially transformative pedagogy, seen in the cases explored in this book, involves deep work in preparation and an ongoing process of creative invention, rebuilding, and transforming of the classroom culture and experiences. Teachers who are truly committed to Freire's (1970) principle of allowing students to "read the world" while "reading the word" must be willing to challenge themselves and their colleagues constantly, in ways such as these:

- examining one's own identity, what brought the teacher to this place, what challenges and hopes she brings.
- exploring the ways that white privilege is structured into every aspect of US society and how to challenge it.
- recognizing the community cultural capital—the assets in discourse, critical thinking, and solidarity—that students bring from their communities.
- committing to a process of constant research, reflection, and action.
- advancing accountability to the community and the needs that oppressed peoples have for new approaches, institutions, and initiatives that advance their surviving and thriving.
- rethinking assessment to give well-rounded, meaningful feedback to students and teachers on the ways classroom knowledge is advancing.
- struggling for social justice, for a world as it could be—free of white supremacy, patriarchy, and class oppression.
- addressing trauma through both trauma-informed teaching and support for the challenges teachers face.

MOVING FORWARD IN TEACHER EDUCATION

Teacher preparation programs that are designed to place new educators in urban schools must have an intentional way of ensuring that teachers are able to engage in self-care, practice affirmations, and discuss the challenges of working in a profession that can be excessively isolating and oppressive. They must learn from and work in solidarity with grassroots organizations that prioritize critical consciousness, professional well-being, and pedagogical growth.

Institutionalizing care and support—not only instructional but also financial and social—are imperative foundations of paving the pathway towards full time K–12 teaching. These are the things that help sustain teachers, that fuel their sense of purpose, and that combat the de-intellectualization and isolation of teaching.

Alongside teacher education, the teaching profession must begin to prioritize this personal development and care through a mix of reflection, self-care, and coalition building. One way to do this is to begin to leverage the existing language and structural responsibilities that states—as the employers of public school teachers—need to own. For example, of the California Standards for the Teaching Profession (CSTP), the sixth and final standard demands of each teacher to "develop as a professional educator." If teacher educators seek to dismantle the attack on teaching, they must place first a teacher's development so as to encourage the kind of reflection, collaboration, community engagement, and purposeful growth articulated within the standard.

The case studies in the book show that these young teachers are professionals—they are dedicated to their craft, they work hard at improving their practice, and they truly love and believe in their students. Additionally, these professionals are committed to a type of education and an educational system that is fundamentally different from the one that exists now. The action research projects and classroom interactions in the subsequent chapters showcase these teachers' journeys towards socially transformative pedagogy and a world in which their students can create the change they desire in their own communities.

The journeys for these teachers are just beginning and the quest for a more equitable educational system is never over. The UESJ program is a part of this quest and it too is a work in progress. Learning from teachers like those highlighted in this book is the most energizing and impactful part of this process, as it shows that there is hope for students in our public schools.

KEY IDEAS IN THIS CHAPTER

- Urban teachers, labeled as ineffective, incompetent, and even lazy, have become scapegoats for the prevailing economic and social issues in the United States. As a result, teachers' unions have also been under attack.
- Teachers are under attack both professionally, with top-down practices like standardized testing, and personally, as they jeopardize their health, financial security, and emotional well-being through unsustainable working conditions.
- Teachers, teacher educators, and urban school professional development must leverage relationships and resources to maintain and sustain the

health and wellness of teachers when addressing the socially toxic stress of schooling.
- Powerful teacher education must subvert institutions whose purpose is to reproduce inequity and must build socially transformative pedagogy.
- The UESJ program and the action research projects highlighted in this book are examples of the quest toward socially transformative pedagogy.

References

Akom, A. A. (2003). Reexamining resistance as oppositional behavior: The Nation of Islam and the creation of black achievement ideology. *Sociology of Education, 76*(4), 305–325.

Atwell, N. (1987). *In the middle.* Portsmouth, NH: Heinemann Press.

Au, Wayne. (2012). Quoted in Hagopian, J. Occupy Education v. the Gates Foundation, *Counterpunch*, March 14, 2012. https://www.counterpunch.org/2012/03/14/occupy-education-v-the-gates-foundation/.

Aviv, R. (2014, July 21). Wrong answer. *The New Yorker*, pp. 54–65.

Ayers, W., Laura, C., & Ayers, R. (2018) *You can't fire the bad ones: And 18 other myths about teachers, teachers' unions, and public education.* Boston, MA: Beacon Press.

Bartolome, L. (1994). Beyond the methods fetish: Toward a humanizing pedagogy. *Harvard Educational Review, 64*, pp. 173–94.

Berliner & Glass, G. (2014). *50 Myths & lies that are threatening America's public schools.* New York, NY: Teachers College Press.

Borrero, N. E., Flores, E., & De La Cruz, G. (2016). Developing and enacting culturally relevant pedagogy: Voices of new teachers of color. *Equity & Excellence in Education, 49*(1), 27–40.

Brion-Meisels, G., Cooper, K., Deckman, S., Dobbs, C., Francois, C., Nikundiwe, T., & Shalaby, C. (Eds.) (2010). Part 1: Insurrectionary generation "the discipline of the radical alternative." In *Humanizing education.* Cambridge, MA: Harvard Educational Review.

Bronfenbrenner, U. (1979). *The ecology of human development.* Cambridge, MA: Harvard University Press.

Carver-Thomas, D., & Darling-Hammond, L. (2017). *Teacher turnover: Why it matters and what we can do about it.* Palo Alto, CA: Learning Policy Institute.

Cobb, C. (1963). "Proposal for a Summer Freedom School Program in Mississippi." Student Non-Violent Coordinating Committee (SNCC) in *Education and Democracy*. Retrieved from http://educationanddemocracy.org/FSCfiles/B_05_ProspForFSchools.htm.

Cosby, B. (2004). Address at the NAACP on the 50th Anniversary of Brown v. Board of Education. *American Rhetoric Online Speech Bank Roots of Language.*

Darling-Hammond, L., Furger, R., Shields, P. M., & Sutcher, L. (2016). Addressing California's emerging teacher shortage: An analysis of sources and solutions, Palo Alto, CA: Learning Policy Institute.

Diamond, J. (2008). Midwinter doldrums and quarrels. In *Kindergarten: A teacher, her students, and a year of learning* (pp. 131–56). New York, NY: The New Press.

Dewey, J. (1910). *The influence of Darwin on philosophy and other essays.* New York, NY: Henry Holt and Company.

Duncan-Andrade, J. M. R. (2007). Gangstas, wankstas, and ridas: Defining, developing, and supporting effective teachers in urban schools. *International Journal of Qualitative Studies in Education, 20*(6), 617–38.

Facella, M. A., Rampino, K. M., & Shea, E. K. (2005). Effective teaching strategies for English language learners. *Bilingual Research Journal, 29*(1), 209–21.

Farmer, P. E., Nizeye, B., Stulac, S., & Keshavjee, S. (2006). Structural violence and clinical medicine. *PLoS medicine, 3*(10), e449.

Feagin, J. R., & Vera, H. (1995). *White racism: The basics.* New York, NY: Routledge.

Freire, P. (1970/2002). *Pedagogy of the oppressed* (30th Anniversary Edition). New York, NY: Continuum.

Freire, P. (1970/1988). The adult literacy process as cultural action for freedom and education and conscientização. In E. R. Kingten, B. Kroll, & M. Rose (Eds.), *Perspectives on literacy* (pp. 398–409). Carbondale, IL: Southern Illinois University Press.

Freire, P. (1998). *Pedagogy of freedom: Ethics, democracy, and civic courage.* Lanham, MD: Rowman & Littlefield.

Freire, P., & Macedo, D. (1987). *Literacy: Reading the word and the world.* Westport, CT: Bergin & Garvey.

Foucault, M. (1977). *Discipline and punishment: The birth of the prison.* New York, NY: Pantheon Books.

Ginwright, S. (2016). *Hope and healing in urban education.* New York, NY: Routledge.

Giroux, H. A. (1988). *Teachers as intellectuals: Toward a critical pedagogy of learning.* Westport, CT: Greenwood Publishing Group.

Giroux, H. (1992). Post-colonial ruptures and democratic possibilities: Multiculturalism as anti-racist pedagogy. *Cultural Critique, 21,* 5–40.

Goodwin, A. L. (2010). Curriculum as colonizer: (Asian) American education in the current U.S. context. *Teachers College Record, 112*(12), 3102–138.

Gutierrez, K. (2008). Developing a socio-critical literacy in the third space. *Reading Research Quarterly, 43,* 148–64.

Haberman, M. (2010). The pedagogy of poverty versus good teaching. *Phi Delta Kappan, 92*(2), 81–87.

Hagopian, J. (2014). A brief history of the "testocracy," standardized testing and test-defying. In Hagopian, Ravitch, & Kohn, *More Than a Score: The New Uprising against High-Stakes Testing.* Chicago, IL: Haymarket Books.

hooks, b. (2010). *Understanding patriarchy.* Louisville, KY: Louisville Anarchist Federation Federation.

Howard, T. C. (2002). Hearing footsteps in the dark: African American students' descriptions of effective teachers. *Journal of Education for Students Placed at Risk, 7,* 425–44.

Hyland, N. E. (2000). *Threatening discourse: Cultural and contextual challenges in constructing antiracist narrative and action in one elementary school.* Unpublished doctoral dissertation retrieved from http://wwwlib.umi.com/dissertations/. University of Illinois at Urbana-Champaign.

Kailin, J. (1999). How white teachers perceive the problem of racism in their schools: A case study in "liberal" Lakeview. *Teachers College Record, 100*(4), 724–50.

Kemmis, S. (2011). A self-reflective practitioner and a new definition of critical participatory action research. In N. Mockler, & J. Sachs (Eds.), *Rethinking educational practice through reflexive inquiry* (Vol. 7, 11–30). Netherlands: Springer.

Kincheloe, J. L. (2008). *Critical pedagogy primer.* New York, NY: Peter Lang.

Kohl, H. (1994). *"I won't learn from you": And other thoughts on creative maladjustment.* New York, NY: Norton & Norton.

Kolbert, E. (2014, March 3). Big score: When Mom takes the SATs. *The New Yorker.* Retrieved from https://www.newyorker.com/magazine/2014/03/03/big-score.

Kumashiro, K. K. (2012). *Bad teacher: How blaming teachers distorts the bigger picture.* New York, NY: Teachers College Press.

Ladson-Billings, G. (1994/2009). *The dreamkeepers: Successful teaching for African-American students.* San Francisco, CA: Jossey-Bass.

Ladson-Billings, G. (1995). But that's just good teaching! The case for culturally relevant pedagogy. *Theory into practice, 34*(3), 159–65.

Ladson-Billings, G. (2006). From the achievement gap to the education debt: Understanding achievement in US schools. *Educational researcher, 35*(7), 3–12.

Ladson-Billings, G. (2016). "#Literate lives matter": Black reading, writing, speaking, and listening in the 21st century. *Literacy Research: Theory, Method, and Practice, 65*(1), 141–51.

Leonardo, Z. (2004). The color of supremacy: Beyond the discourse of "white privilege." *Educational Philosophy and Theory, 36*(2): 137–52.

Levin, M., Kessler, H. M., Stratton, R. (Producers), & Levin, M. (Director). (1998). *Slam* [Motion picture]. United States: Trimark Pictures.

Lippman, W. (1922 October) The mental age of Americans. *New Republic, 32*: 213–15

Lorde, A. (1984). *Sister outsider: Essays and speeches.* Trumansburg, NY: The Crossing Press.

MacLeod, J. (1987). *Ain't no makin' it: Aspirations and attainment in a low-income neighborhood.* Boulder, CO: Westview Press.

McIntosh, P. (1988). *White privilege and male privilege: A personal account of coming to see correspondences through work in women's studies.* Wellesley, MA: Wellesley College, Center for Research on Women.

McLaren, P. (1994/2003). *Life in schools: An introduction to critical pedagogy in the foundations of education* (2nd ed.). New York, NY: Longman.

McLaren, P. (2000). *Che Guevara, Paulo Freire, and the pedagogy of revolution.* Lanham, MD: Rowman & Littlefield.

Meier, D., & Knoester, M. (2017) *Beyond testing.* New York, NY: Teachers College Press.

Mertler, C. A. (2012). *Action research: Improving schools and empowering educators.* Thousand Oaks, CA: Sage.

Nasir, N. S., & Saxe, G. B. (2003). Emerging tensions and their management in the lives of minority students. *Educational Researcher, 32*(5), 14–18.

National Center for Educational Statistics (2018). Retrieved December 12 2018 from https://nces.ed.gov/pubs2009/2009324/tables/sass0708_2009324_t12n_02.asp.

Newton, H. (1971). *Revolutionary suicide.* New York, NY: Penguin Books.

Nieto, S. (2002). Introduction: Language literacy and culture: intersections and implications. In S. Nieto, *Language, culture, and teaching: Critical perspectives for a new century* (pp. 1–24). New York, NY: Routledge.

Paris, D., & Alim, H. S. (2014). What are we seeking to sustain through culturally sustaining pedagogy? A loving critique forward. *Harvard Educational Review, 84*(1), 85–100.

Payne, R., DeVol, P., & Smith, T. R. (2001). *Bridges out of poverty: Strategies for professionals and communities.* Highlands, TX: aha! Process, Inc.

Payne, R. (2005). *A framework for understanding poverty.* Highlands, TX: aha! Process, Inc.

Pearlstein, L. (2008). *Tested: One American school struggles to make the grade.* New York, NY: Henry Holt and Company.

Perry, T., Steele, C., & Hilliard, A. (2003). *Young, gifted and black: Promoting high achievement among African-American students.* Boston, MA: Beacon Press.

Pratt, R. H. (1892). Official Report of the Nineteenth Annual Conference of Charities and Correction. In *Americanizing the American Indians: Writings by the "Friends of the Indian" 1880–1900* (1973). Cambridge, MA: Harvard University Press.

Rothstein, R. (2015, April 3). Taking the fall in Atlanta. *Economic Policy Institute*. Retrieved July 21, 2018 from https://www.epi.org/blog/taking-the-fall-in-atlanta/.

Sitting Bull. (1883). Native American Rights Fund Announcements. *National Indian Law Library, 2*(1), 1–30. Retrieved September 3, 2019, from https://www.narf.org/nill/documents/nlr/nlr2-1.pdf.

Solorzano, D. G., & Yosso, T. J. (2001). From racial stereotyping and deficit discourse toward a critical race theory of teacher education. *Multicultural Education, 9*, 2–8.

Solorzano, D. G., & Yosso, T. J. (2002). Critical race methodology: Counter-storytelling as an analytical framework for education research. *Qualitative Inquiry, 8*(1), 23–44.

Spring, J. (2004). *Deculturalization and the struggle for equality* (4th ed.). New York, NY: McGraw Hill.

References

Stanley, S. A. (1998). Empathic caring in classroom management and discipline. In R. Butchart & B. McEwan (Eds.), *Classroom discipline in American schools problems and possibilities for democratic education* (pp. 237–68). Albany, NY: State University of New York.

Stefanakis, E. H. (2000). Teacher's judgments do count: Assessing bilingual students. In Reykont, J. F. (Ed.), *Lifting every voice*. Cambridge, MA: Harvard Education Publishing Group.

Trump, D. (2000). *The America we deserve*. Los Angeles, CA: Renaissance Books.

Valenzuela, A. (1999). *Subtractive schooling: U.S.-Mexican youth and the politics of caring*. New York, NY: SUNY Press.

Vygotsky, L. S. (1978). *Mind in society: The development of higher psychological processes*. Cambridge, MA: Harvard University Press.

Yang, K. W. (2009). Discipline or punish? Some suggestions for school policy and teacher practice. *Language Arts, 87*(1), 49–61.

Yosso, T. J. (2005). Whose culture has capital? A critical race theory discussion of community cultural wealth. *Race Ethnicity and Education, 8*(1), 69–91.

Watkins, W. (2001). *The white architects of black education, 1865–1954*. New York, NY: Teachers College Press.

Westervelt, E. (2015). Where have all the teachers gone? Retrieved from http://www.npr.org/blogs/ed/2015/03/03/389282733/where-have-all-the-teachers-gone.

Willis, P. (1977). *Learning to labour: How working class kids get working class jobs*. Farnborough, England: Saxon House.

Wilson, C. (1970). Racism in Education, in B. N. Schwartz and R. Disch, *White racism: Its history, pathology, and practice*. New York, NY: Dell Publishers.

Woodson, C. G. (1933). *The mis-education of the negro*. New York: AMS Press.

Woodson, C. G. (2000). *The miseducation of the negro*. Chicago, IL: African-American Images.

Zinn, H. (2003/1980). *A people's history of the United States: 1492–2001*. New York, NY: Harper Collins.

Zinn, H. (2009). *A young people's history of the United States: Columbus to the War on Terror*. New York: Penguin Books.

About the Authors

Noah Borrero's scholarship is grounded in the belief that the cultural strengths of communities provide unique opportunities for teaching, learning, and social transformation. He teaches courses in bilingual education, critical pedagogy, action research, learning theory, and teaching for diversity and social justice.

Patrick Roz Camangian engages in grassroots and professional efforts to advocate for humanizing, socially transformative education as a university professor, district- and school-based educator, and community organizer. Currently, he is turning to both critical theory and research in the health sciences to inform his research findings on systemic harm, social resistance, and health and well-being in education.

Rick Ayers's research and writing focuses on social justice and critical pedagogy in education. He is author or coauthor of a number of books, including *Teaching the Taboo, An Empty Seat in Class: Teaching and Learning After the Death of a Student,* and *You Can't Fire the Bad Ones: And 18 Other Myths about Teachers, Teachers Unions, and Public Education.*

Sharim Hannegan-Martinez is a first-generation doctoral candidate in education at UCLA. Her research, which is heavily influenced by her experiences as a Chicana growing up on the San Diego/Tijuana border and her time as a teacher in Oakland, focuses primarily on the role of loving relationships in helping young people cope with, navigate, and heal from traumatic stressors in the context of urban classrooms.

Esther Flores is a teacher committed to continuously improving her practice in order to provide young people with a relevant and rigorous education that empowers them to build a more just society. She currently teaches ethnic studies and world history at Mission High School in San Francisco. She earned her master's degree in teaching and single-subject bilingual social science teaching credential from the urban education and social justice program at the University of San Francisco in 2014.

www.ingramcontent.com/pod-product-compliance
Lightning Source LLC
Chambersburg PA
CBHW030144240426
43672CB00005B/262